WHAT OTHERS

"Simple yet thought-provo[king]... companion in a journey of transforming mindsets and changing lives" — **Grace De Castro**, HR Expert, Mavericus People Management

"A must-read for every Filipino who wants change, simply life-changing!" — **Edgar Bella Agustin**, Continuous Improvement Manager, Toppan Best-Set Pre-Media Limited

"Truly heartwarming! Packed with actionable tips to live an empowered life to the fullest." — **Celine Francisco**, Content Strategy Consultant & Co-Author of "Cyberpreneur Philippines"

"Full of hope and wisdom, the next generation has to learn from it." — **Marlon Molmisa**, Inspirational Speaker & Author

"This book is a challenge to each one of us, that in our own little way, we can contribute something for the benefit of our country" — **Dr. Shirard Leonardo C. Adiviso**, Director, Asian Hospital and Medical Center & Professor, De La Salle Health Sciences Institute

"This book is as demanding as my grade school teacher. It wants you to think, inspires you to dream, encourages you to feel, and forces you to act. Expect change by the last page. The good kind." — **Mar C. Benitez**, Managing Director, Galing Pinoy Community

"When I started reading it, I couldn't stop. A truly inspiring book. It made me reflect deeply about my own purpose in life" — **Gerry Plana**, CEO, Investors in People Philippines

"An easy-to-read, engaging yet challenging book for Pinoys and Pinays and anyone searching for a roadmap towards a life filled with intent and meaning" — **Fr. Renato de Guzman**, Parish Priest, Don Bosco, Makati

WHAT OTHERS HAVE SAID...

"This book made me cry! It is a materpiece! As you start reading it, you will not stop until you realize you are already at the end of the book." — **Leo S. Gellor,** *Vice President, People Management Association of the Philippines*

"A real treasure and a truly inspiring book. A must read for Filipinos who really want a better and brighter future for the Philippines." — **Danny Moran,** *CEO, Amici Restaurants*

"The 7 powerful lessons make such a compelling connection to get to the core of who you really are and who you want to become." — **Jenn Galvez,** *Founder of Boto Ko Sagrado & Barangay Tapat advocacies*

"THE RISE OF THE PINOY is a force to reckon with. It will go down in history as one of the most important Filipino entrepreneurial and motivational books! It is a thought-provoking, step-by-step program for those who want to embark on a journey of personal awakening and holistic development." — **Charina Villa,** *Clarin Real Estate Proprietor, ESL Teacher and Blogger*

"I believe the Philippines is on the verge of a renaissance. The Rise of the Pinoy is loaded with heart-warming stories and practical advice to inspire any Filipino who wants to be a part of it. This is your time. This book is your guide." — **Mark Joyner,** *Founder of Simpleology and #1 Bestselling author of a dozen books in print in 25 languages*

"Inspirational in the best way possible, showcasing great successes and the sensational ambition of our fellow countrymen to draw on as inspiration in our everyday lives." — **Nathan Riskin,** *Business Development Officer, Mitsui & Co.*

"Easy-to-read, this book offers a clear step-by-step guide to building a life filled with purpose and passion." — **Tom Graham,** *Best-Selling Author, "Genius of the Poor"*

WHAT OTHERS HAVE SAID...

"The Rise of the Pinoy is a book that speaks directly to its readers. It is very straight to the point and pierces right through one's comfort zone. It is a must-read for those who are struggling in love, career, or any aspect in life. After reading this book, you will feel like a phoenix, stronger, and better than your last version of you."
— **Karmela Mirriam Queen**, *Blogger at www.mirriamdictionary.wordpress.com*

"A short yet powerful book, really worth reading. Each chapter is a journey. No word is wasted." — **Monica Shiena Sagad**, *Certified Speech Pathologist and Speaker*

"More than just a source of inspiration, the book is an amazing way to see the potential of the Filipino in a different perspective. This is a book you bring with you while you grow—assisting you to always be on your track to success." — **Syrene Dy Correa**, *Event Director*

"Not your typical book, with its inspiring stories to emulate and actionable challenges to apply, this book will empower every Filipino to 7x growth." — **RM Nisperos**, *UPOU E-Commerce Professor*

"Brimming with real stories that show how it is to go against what is popular and traditional. It's a powerful tool that will see you off and egg you on in your search for fulfillment." — **Jose Roberto Del Rosario**, *President, LifeQuest Training*

"A book that will make you truly proud you are Pinoy. The stories are not only stories of inspiration but also stories that will challenge you to step up and do your part as a Filipino. It will make you take action." — **JM Matienzo**, *CEO & President, Ariva Events Management*

"The Rise of the Pinoy is perfect for the Filipino go-getter who strives to not just have ideas to reach success but execute them to meet their goals." — **Kristel Joy Silang**, *Content Marketer and Co-Author of Cyberpreneur Philippines*

© Copyright 2016

THE RISE OF THE PINOY
Mike Grogan

ISBN 978-621-95461-0-2

Author: Mike Grogan, www.mikegrogan.ph

Edited by: Penelope Cabot

Published by: Art Angel Printshop Commercial Quests Inc.

All rights reserved.

No part of this publication may be reproduced, except for brief quotations, without the prior permission of the author.

Dedication

To the Overseas Filipino Workers (OFWs), and the extraordinary value you have given the world. **Thank you.**

Supporting Nation Building

10% of all author royalties from this book are donated to Gawad Kalinga

GAWAD KALINGA
www.gk1world.com

The Mission of this book

Our mission is to get this book into the hands of over a million Filipinos around the world to help them on their journey of realizing their greatness.
We believe that every Pinoy is capable and worthy of becoming world-class. We passionately believe that, when this potential is unleashed, we will see a First World Philippines in our lifetime. Thank you so much for your support! ☺

TABLE OF CONTENTS

Foreword 1

Before We Begin 7

A Special Invitation 14

Chapters

    1 Find Your Inspiration 15

    2 Your Unique Assignment 29

    3 Discover Your Motivation 43

    4 Your Greatest Enemy 59

    5 Embrace Your Pain. 71

    6 Your Daily Victory 89

    7 You were Born for Greatness 103

The 40-Day Challenge 121

Book Summary 129

Epilogue 131

Acknowledgements 133

About the Author 135

One Last Thing 136

FOREWORD

World-class Filipinos, World-class Philippines

The Best Filipino Global Brand is the Filipino himself. This book by Mike Grogan is a celebration of the excellence of this brand. The Filipino brand is known for outstanding service to humanity. It includes the best health providers in America; the toughest engineers in the most remote oilfields and minefields in the coldest and hottest regions of the earth; skilled sailors navigating the seas for maritime commerce; popular entertainers in the plushiest of clubs and luxury liners. Even Filipino nannies are at the top of their field for their nurturing nature, according to Malaysian and French employers I have met.

Love of Family Fuels Heroism

Love of family is often the greatest driver for Filipinos to dare, and endure life's greatest challenges: cold winters in Canada; abusive employers in the Middle East or the pain of separation from, and for the sake of, loved ones. Ironically, they will leave their children to take care of foreign children abroad so their biological children will have a better life in the poor communities they have left behind.

> The Best Filipino Global Brand is the Filipino himself

The best professionals, consultants, corporate executives and scientists from the Philippines will seek opportunities abroad because we have not used our skills to create opportunities at home. Coming from a long colonial past followed by elite globalization, our education has prepared us to be competitive as jobseekers abroad, but not job givers at home. We are consumers of inferior foreign goods, not producers of world-class products at home. Our long history of subservience to foreign masters has made us resilient to adversity but not yet confident enough to be masters of our undeveloped industries and owners of multinational corporations. But Filipinos thrive if the environment is right.

Filipino Excellence

In the US, I've witnessed the capacity of Filipinos to compete in a meritocracy that rewards competence and hard work. They live well, becoming successful doctors and nurses who've hosted me in palatial homes and are good citizens and taxpayers.

They are averse to accepting handouts. I did not meet a Filipino among the homeless in Seattle or San Francisco where I did some research. It is not in our nature to be the object of charity if the environment rewards self-reliance and honors self-respect. They give back to our country generously: the work of Gawad Kalinga flourished due to massive support from Filipinos abroad who have not stopped caring for our people.

Filipinos thrive if the environment is right.

Even at home, we continue to serve humanity as the call center capital of the world. The gracious voices with the quaintest English accents - sometimes with a trace of an Ilonggo singsong or whatever dialects are native -that reach many homes and offices abroad are those of Filipinos from Luzon, Visayas and Mindanao who have become effective communicators and connectors in the BPO world.

Two revenue streams, remittances from OFWs and income from our BPO industry, have kept our economy afloat in the last two decades, contributing $25 billion apiece annually, helping to make the Philippines the second fastest rising economy in the world according to Bloomberg in 2015. While Filipinos have proven their worth in various professions in the Philippines and abroad, there are other fields of opportunity for us to explore, master and conquer. Two of them are technology and agriculture.

Love of Country at the Heart of Business

Technology is not yet our game. But we'll get there. We have no Toyota or Sony like the Japanese, no Hyundai or Samsung like the South Koreans. These Asian brands are known all over the world. They compete with the best that America and Europe can produce and contribute significantly to their country's economy and to their people's image of excellence in the field of technology.

The Japanese and South Korean economies grew out of extreme adversity: the Japanese from their defeat in the Second World War 70 years ago; the South Koreans after barely surviving the fight with their Northern Communist kin in the late 50s, with a little help from Filipino soldiers and other international sympathizers in the years when the world was polarized by the Cold War.

Their economies rose from the bottom with a strong work culture anchored on integrity and honor. National pride created a patriotic market for their products and services and a solidarity economy that did not foster a crab mentality. Poverty did not make them a slave to mediocrity. In the beginning "Made in Japan" or "Made in Korea" meant inferior and cheap in the global market but they just kept trying and getting better over the years. Now many of their brands are market leaders. Business prospered because the solid foundation was love of country.

Building an Inclusive Philippine Economy

The world will continue to demand the services of top Filipino professionals, but the Philippines will soon shift towards new pathways for inclusive wealth creation at home, particularly in the field of agri-business, manufacturing and social tourism. The local Millennials, who are now more connected to global excellence, humanitarian conscience and plain commonsense through social media and travel, are becoming more daring as social innovators and business pioneers, seeing the bottom of the pyramid, particularly the rural areas, as the undiscovered, unexplored, undeveloped minefield of human gems and gold in the fertile land.

With the phenomenal success of the movie General Luna about Filipino heroism, the massive growth of the Gawad Kalinga movement for nation-building and the increasing patronage for local brands like Human Nature - which is anchored on a Pro-Philippines, Pro-poor and Pro-environment campaign - there appears to be a clear trend towards the development of a patriotic and socially conscious market. Human Nature as a social enterprise has niched itself as the leading brand in the Philippines in the field of natural cosmetics and personal care products, with 150 products visible in retail outlets nationwide and available on-line, and is currently expanding its marketing network in North America, the Middle East and Southeast Asia.

> The world will continue to demand the services of top Filipino professionals

Creating Shared Prosperity

With its success in scalability and sustainability, Gawad Kalinga, the womb that bore Human Nature, is confidently incubating more brands in various industries: low-hanging fruits in food and beverage, hospitality and tourism, essential oils, fragrances, toys, and health products with a consciousness for higher quality over popular imported brands.

To capture and promote this trend, it is building the first Farm Village University at the GK Enchanted Farm in Angat, Bulacan, as a hub and ecosystem for Social business start-ups. Its goal is to replicate this in 24 other provinces and to raise 500,000 social entrepreneurs in 10 years, creating jobs and profit to help improve the lives of 5 million Filipinos.

> This book is a lens, roadmap and compass to this goal

Big Filipino brands like San Miguel, Jollibee and Unilab are market leaders locally and growing globally, catering to the taste and nostalgia of 11 million OFWs and expats. The challenge for them is to be mainstream global brands like Nestlé, Coca Cola, MacDonalds and Unilever.

But the more exciting investment of Filipino excellence is in the field of social entreneurship with the clear and concrete goal of ending poverty in the Philippines by creating shared prosperity. This is possible within the next decade if we raise a new generation of Filipinos, with foreign partners who genuinely care for our country, working together to build a "walang iwanan" economy, creating abundance for all out of love for family, country and the rest of humanity. This book is a lens, roadmap and compass to this goal.

Tony Meloto
Founder of Gawad Kalinga
www.gk1world.com

BEFORE WE BEGIN

Why I wrote this book

What is this Irish guy doing here in the Philippines? It is a question I get asked almost every day. In 2013, after living in Europe, America and Africa, I had a strong desire to move to Asia. I was hungry to discover the world but, more importantly, I was looking for a place where I could grow and contribute the most. I thought: why not start in the Philippines? After all, I have met Filipinos in almost every country I have traveled through and was really impressed by their character.

I began to learn that our countries have so much in common. We were both colonized, we are both strongly influenced by the Roman Catholic Church, and we both have a history of mass immigration. More powerful were the similarities in our people: friendly; family-oriented; determined and, of course, we are both very good-looking people! ☺

After only a few days in the Philippines, I could hear a voice deep inside me telling me that this is where I need to be; that a unique assignment was waiting for me here; that I was to play a significant part in serving the Filipino people. A part of this unique assignment is the book you are reading now.

World-Class Filipinos

A few months after arriving, I decided that I would start my own Podcast: "The Best of You" Podcast. As part of the podcast, I conducted in-depth interviews with people who loved the Philippines and were doing something extraordinary to add value to its people. The success of the podcast blew me away. It became one of the most listened - to podcasts in the country.

I was fortunate that almost all of the people I requested to meet and interview said 'yes'. It is their stories that really make this book so special. Some are famous, others you may have never heard of, but the one thing I observed in all of them is that they all made a decision to be intentional with their life. They were all committed to becoming the best version of themselves. As you will soon read, their decision to develop themselves not only changed their world but also enabled them to make a significant, lasting impact on the lives of countless others. This is what makes them world-class. In this book, I will share some of the most inspiring stories and most profound insights I took from interviewing 21 of these world-class Filipinos.

Who this book is written for

This book is written for you! It is written to give you a very important message about the extraordinary power that lies within you. This book will show you exactly what you need to do to become world-class; to unleash your potential; to realize your greatness. If the people featured in this book can achieve so much success, so can you. Books have played a significant role in my personal development. But every so often comes a book that changes everything. If you fully embrace this book, it will not only change how you look at your life but will also change the way you live your life. So keep your mind alert. Keep your heart receptive. Never forget that this book is written for you.

How you should read this book

Most people do not know how to read effectively. I don't want you to make that mistake. If you are truly to see the full transformational impact of this book, I want you to follow the 3 steps below:

1. **Read with a pen**: I can't emphasize enough the power of note taking when it comes to acquiring new knowledge. You will be 10 times more likely to remember what you read if you actively take notes as you go. Scientifically proven. If you look at any of the books that I have read, it is full of underlines, side notes, reflections, ideas and commentary. This is what I want you to do. You can write in the book itself, in a notebook, or type on your phone: whatever works best for you. As an added bonus, if you read with a pen in your hand you can also use the pen to guide your eyes as you read each line. This simple technique is used by some of the smartest people in the world to increase their reading speed by 20-30%. Trust me on this. Read with a pen!

2. **Do the Exercises**: At the end of each of the chapters is a 5 Minute Challenge. Yes, you heard me correctly. If this is the book that will change your life, you must complete each of the challenges. It will only take you 5 minutes! The primary purpose of each chapter is for you to complete the 5 Minute Challenge. The most powerful question you must ask yourself after each chapter is -"What does this mean to me?". Completing each challenge will help you significantly. It will allow you to maximize the value you get from this book. Knowing without doing is not knowing. Understanding without doing is not understanding. Learning without doing is not learning. Please do not skip this: it matters.

3. **Share with someone**: Think of someone in your life you care deeply about who is going through a difficult time right now. A best friend, a family member, or a work colleague. Perhaps it is someone you know who has got so much potential and who would be really inspired by the stories in this book. Or perhaps

it is someone who is really hungry to realize his or her greatness but is feeling stuck. I want you to share with this person the stories from this book that you think will really help them. One of the greatest lessons I've learned in life is that you can't make it on your own. This simple act of sharing a story with someone may have a massive impact on how they think. Also, every time you share, it will help you understand more profoundly how you can apply the lesson to your own life. Everyone wins. So, as you finish each chapter, always ask yourself – "who would benefit from hearing this story?"

Your companions on this journey

You will not be alone when you read this book. I have asked two readers, **Lucy** and **Diego**, to share their experiences with you as they go through this book. We have changed their names to protect their identity. They have both shown tremendous vulnerability in sharing their experiences with you. You will read how they completed each of the exercises. It took a lot of courage for them to write what they did and even more courage to share these experiences with you! They are here to inspire you. They are here to empower you. They have led the way: I expect you to follow.

So let's learn more about **Lucy** and **Diego**

Lucy, 24	Diego, 27
Lucy works as a part time call center agent and is the youngest of 4 siblings. She is a single mom to a 3-year old girl named Erika. Lucy loves to learn and has a passion for children's education. Lucy volunteers at a local non-profit group that helps empower disadvantaged youth. She dreams of a day where all Filipino children get access to an excellent education.	Diego is a young professional from a family of engineers. Diego loves kart-racing and playing the guitar. He dreams of being a rockstar! He is the lead guitarist in his band but he says that this is not the way his dad sees him in the future. He has a younger brother who is expected to settle down soon. To quote Diego: "All the pressure's on me", since he is expected to take over their family business.

Lucy	Diego
What are your expectations from reading this book?	
I hope this book can inspire me more to figure out what I am going to do with my life. I have lots of ideas but I am not sure what is for me. Maybe it might help me in other areas of my life, to be a better mom for Erika?	*I don't know. I don't know how exactly it will help me. Perhaps it will help me become more productive at work. Not sure.*
Who's the first person you are going to share the stories from this book to?	
Nica – she's one of my best friends. We volunteer together every weekend.	*Joseph – he is one of the guys at work.*
Why did you choose that person?	
Because Nica is like me. She is smart and I know she has potential. I see her get easily discouraged sometimes and it frustrates me when I can't help her.	*Joseph is one of the guys I really connect with at work. Although we spend most of our time talking about sports, we do have the occasional deep conversation. I think he would appreciate this. Also like me, he is not in love with his job so I hope it can benefit him.*

The 5 Minute Challenge - Your Turn!

What are your expectations from reading this book?

Who's the first person you are going to share the stories from this book to?

Why did you choose that person?

A Note from Mike...

So have you completed the exercise? You sure? I am going to be very strict with you because I really want you to experience this book like you have never experienced any other book before. This book was written for you. I don't want you even to read the next chapter if you have not completed the exercise. It is *that* important. At the end of the book you will understand why. At the end of the book you will see how valuable doing these exercises are. Thank you for trusting me. Now let **The Rise of the Pinoy** begin!

A Special Invitation

I would like to personally invite you to join
"The Rise of the Pinoy Community" (on Facebook).
This is a special group only for people who have read this book and want to experience a new way of living their life.

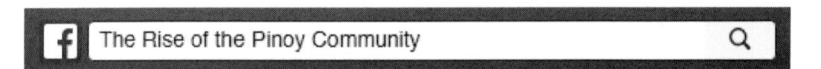

| f | The Rise of the Pinoy Community | 🔍 |

My team and I will be posting additional bonus materials that we promise will support you as you accelerate your journey to becoming world-class.

One of the most important lessons I have learned in life is that, if we are to realize our greatness, we cannot make it on our own. This community is here to help you. *Join us today*!

See you there,

Mike ☺

CHAPTER 1

Find Your Inspiration

Who inspires you to become a better person? Is there someone in your life who has made a significant positive impact on you? Is there someone, without whose love, sacrifice and wisdom, you would not be where you are today? Someone who has shaped who you are today? Think really deeply about this. That person may be a parent, a grandparent, an older brother, a boss or a close friend. Or what about the great men and women from the past? Is there someone from history who has made extraordinary sacrifices for the greater good that you greatly admire? That person may be a national hero like Jose Rizal, have demonstrated an abundance of love like Mother Theresa, or have been a force of freedom like Nelson Mandela. Or is there someone from today's world of business, entertainment or philanthropy that you greatly admire? Someone who has achieved great success. Someone who makes you step back and applaud.

"Who inspires you?" This is a question that I have asked to every one of the world-class Filipinos I interviewed for this book. To understand how people have achieved great success in life, we must be able to deconstruct how they were able to achieve that success. I could write an entire book about the sources of inspiration that have helped me on my journey. One person, however, has made an extraordinary impact on me. Her name is Dr. Brenda D'Mello.

Dr. Brenda D'Mello

I spent two years working side by side with Dr. Brenda in the city of Dar Es Salaam, Tanzania.

Whenever I am asked about the proudest moment of my career, it is my work with Dr. Brenda that comes first to my mind. She is my hero. I have never seen someone so passionate about her mission in life than Brenda. In the city of Dar es Salaam, Tanzania, where Brenda lives, 10 babies die unnecessarily every day as a result of complications in childbirth. In her country, 8,000 women every year will die needlessly due to complications in their pregnancy or during childbirth. Dr. Brenda has committed her life to stopping this great human tragedy. Seeing her in action has inspired me beyond words.

Ironically, it was my job to inspire and empower Brenda. I was hired by the hospital to improve the management and leadership skills of the organization's managers. Brenda was one of the managers I was assigned to. However, I am convinced that I have learned more from Brenda than I could have ever given to her. Her journey in life is extraordinary. When she went to university to study medicine, she was one of the few women in the class. Some of her professors even mocked her, telling her she would be better off finding a rich man to marry than pursuing her education. Inspired by the faith, love and belief of her father, Brenda would not allow those words to hold her back. She graduated as a doctor and found her passion in mother and child healthcare. She married and had two children. Life was good. Then tragedy hit:

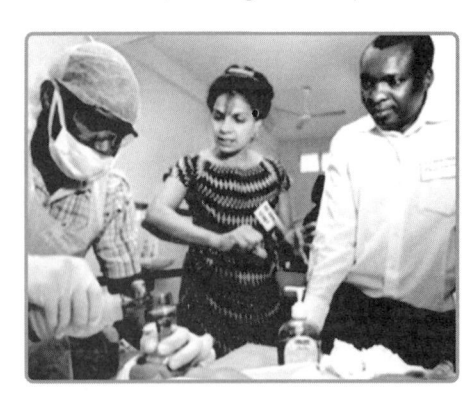

Brenda lost her husband in a car accident and was left to raise her two young children on her own.

The reason I proudly call Dr. Brenda my hero is how she responds to every adversity in her life. Where others would have crumbled, Brenda kept moving forward. Seeing her raise her children, serve in her church and attend to her patients was so inspiring. She showed me the meaning of commitment. I've never met someone so passionate about self-improvement. She became the model manager in the entire hospital. As I write these words it has been over a year since I last saw her. But every day she continues to inspire me. When I think of how I can become more compassionate, more empathetic and more committed, I think of Dr. Brenda and the example she gave. I am so grateful that I got the chance to know her. Let's now look at the stories of three world-class Filipinos and how they found their inspiration to achieve great things.

> Why I proudly call Dr. Brenda my hero is how she responds to every adversity in her life

Josh Mahinay — Founder, Bag 943

In 2012, Josh Mahinay founded BAG 943 (Be a Giver), a social enterprise that designs and manufactures high quality lifestyle bags. What makes the organization so unique is that, for every bag that you and I purchase, another bag is given to a disadvantaged child from one of its adopted public schools across the Philippines. To date, over six thousand children have been impacted by their extraordinary generosity. I sat down with Josh to learn about his amazing story and the inspiration behind BAG 943.

"When I was in Grade 4, I remember living in Zamboanga, Sibugay in Mindanao, one of the poorest provinces in the country. We did not have anything. We are nine in the family so I have eight younger siblings. I remember walking 10

kilometers every day using a plastic bag as a school bag.

I remember that, at lunch time, I would go around the campus just to let time pass. So, when the class resumed, my classmates assumed that I had taken my lunch already but I was just going around because I had nothing to eat. At one point my parents told me to stop going to school.

When I got the chance to really change the situation of my family, of my life, I graduated to help other people. I got a good job and went to the US. In 2011, I came back to the Philippines and I went to the province and I saw this kid going to school using the same type of plastic bag I used when I was little. It's something that really turned my life around, and you know what, God is really up to something. God allowed me to be poor and allowed poverty to be experienced so that I could be in this particular moment and tell a story because, as I always say, we live to tell a story. Some stories we are proud to tell, some stories we talk about. I think, with my story, it gives me an idea that the problem in this country is not really poverty but the mindset that it cannot be changed.

Even in the time I decided to go back home from the States to do Bag 943, a lot of people were talking about me and laughing about my decision. Because a lot of Filipinos would die to get to the United States – that's the land of milk and honey for so many Filipinos. But here I am. I was in the States but I decided to come back in 2012. I realized that life is not

> God allowed me to be poor and allowed poverty to be experienced so that I could be in this particular moment and tell a story

about getting what you want and accomplishing things, but it's really going beyond that and creating an impact in the lives of other people.

> Life is not about getting what you want and accomplishing things, but it's really going beyond that and creating an impact in the lives of other people

It's a little bit funny because a lot of people wouldn't have thought that a poor young boy, who used to live on a mountain, would be in my position right now. My story is not just about a poor kid overcoming poverty: it's really a story of someone going back to his roots to tell a story of how God transformed his life and allowed situations and people to be at the right place at the right time so he could be empowered and empower other people as well."

Francis Kong — Best-Selling Author

Francis Kong is one of the most respected inspirational speakers in the Philippines. He is a best-selling author, a broadcaster, and one of the country's most sought-after Leadership Trainers. Francis has literally inspired millions of Filipinos around the world. I was curious to find out who inspires him.

"People see me as a public figure. I love meeting new friends, I love asking questions, I love learning from people. What they don't really know about me is that I am actually an introvert and everybody in the family is an introvert. In fact, we are close to being anti-social but we love being alone with each other. That's why I don't go to parties. I don't really spend a lot of time doing social activities apart from the fact that they are helpful in achieving goals. I'm a very intense person, concentrated only on things that will add value to my life and to help me reach my success goals. I am a firm believer in the Pareto Principle: that, if I spend a minimum on the few important things and stick to it, it will deliver up to 90 percent of my success goals. However, I'm a hopeless romantic. People see me as analytical but my wife knows me very well. Our marriage is growing stronger now that we are hitting 35 years of being together. She is always with me. I always introduce her as my one and only treasure and treasurer as well! So it is practically impossible for me to function without her.

> I am a firm believer in the Pareto Principle: that, if I spend a minimum on the few important things and stick to it, it will deliver up to 90 percent of my success goals

I get a lot of compliments almost everywhere, especially after speaking to large audiences. I have learned to develop a healthy sense of amnesia by saying 'Thank You Lord, this is your work and not mine alone. Had you not been here, this may not have been possible.' Forget it and concentrate on the next job. But what particularly inspires me is when I have comments like 'You know, Francis, I heard you many years ago and I was failing in school. Now, I am graduating with honors.' And I guess what tops them all is when this young girl sent me a photo of her baby and she said: 'Thank you Francis, for convincing me not to commit suicide and take my own life. She's my joy now. And I thank you for the advice that it would have been a very wrong decision: That I would have killed this baby that I love so much.' For me, that's one of the things that really gave me the most inspiration.

As Filipinos we must become more intentional, we must become more educated, we must become more disciplined. We must unleash the creativity and inspiration that God has given us. We must maintain our virtues of respect for elders and respect for authorities. Never allowing ourselves to be bought. We must become more intelligent, more purposeful and become a blessing not only to this country but to the world."

Krie Reyes Lopez — Founder, Messy Bessy

Krie Reyes Lopez is the founder of Messy Bessy, a manufacturer and wholesaler of natural, chemical-free household and personal care cleaning products made by at-risk young adults who receive skills, education and mentorship to help their rehabilitation into society. I spoke to Krie about what inspired her to take this journey.

"When I look back, my mom used to take me to orphanages when I was four and that made a huge impact on me. My mom was, and remains, an active and committed social worker of some sort, so that also had an impact on me.

> Seeing the young adults in our program every day go against all odds; seeing them persevere and work so hard, and study so hard: that is the inspiration

The reason we established Messy Bessy was to find jobs and an education program for at-risk young adults. At-risk, meaning formerly abused, formerly trafficked, formerly impoverished young adults. This is what has always driven the business. 70 - 80% of our workforce right now are these at-risk young adults and we have an ongoing program that puts all of them through school: high school, college. There are also a lot of other things going on like mentorships and psychological support, and counseling and guidance from everybody involved.

To share one story, let me tell you about Roselyn. She had an extremely traumatic past: I can't even talk about it, it's too much. She's a victim of underage trafficking. Although she was pretty much labeled as fully-recovered by her organization, she came to us very emotionally unstable. At that time, maybe four years ago, she would come to us and she couldn't even talk in front of people. She had to be facing the wall, she had to be holding someone's hand, she would space out. Now, she's already in her third year of college. She's a supervisor for some of the kids and she speaks with so much confidence. She's a complete turnaround, a low-potential one that we're able to help. For me, seeing the young adults in our program every day go against all odds; seeing them persevere and work so hard, and study so hard: that is the inspiration.

People always asked me, 'Why are you doing what you're doing?' because for some people it's just so crazy to dedicate your life to this. My answer was always 'I don't think I'm any more noble than any other person who is pursuing what they want to do.' I'm not any more noble than the dancer who wants to dance, or the architect who wants to design buildings. I don't think I'm any more noble than that. I just want to do what I'm doing. For me it doesn't even feel like work. So I always tell people you have to be true to yourself. For if you are true to yourself, that is where you will be happiest and that is where you will thrive."

> I always tell people you have to be true to yourself. For, if you are true to yourself, that is where you will be happiest and that is where you will thrive

Powerful Lesson # 1
Be reminded of your inspiration daily

Inspiration is simply someone or something that makes you want to become a better person and achieve great things. We all need inspiration: no exceptions. One of the common factors that unites all of the world-class Filipinos in this book is that they did not become world-class overnight: it is a journey. Success in life is a journey. The road ahead is long, unpredictable and full of barriers for you to overcome. No one has ever realized their greatness without being able to tap into their unique source of inspiration. That person or thing that reminds them to get back up when they fall, to keep looking ahead, to keep moving forward.

We have been blessed that we live in a world where there is an abundance of inspiration around us. From seeing the sun rise in the morning, to the smell of fresh air in your lungs, to the sound of birds singing in the trees. I believe that even more powerful inspiration exists in the people who have touched our lives, from the great men and women of history, to our intimate friendships, to the unsung heroes of our communities.

However, our problem is not a lack of inspiration in our lives. Our problem is that we fail to remember. We forget. For the 5 Minute Challenge I want you to deeply understand your own unique source of inspiration, but I also want you to really think creatively of ways that you can be reminded of this inspiration DAILY. We all need to be reminded of our source of inspiration daily. No exceptions. I invite you now to complete the next exercise before moving on to the next chapter.

The 5 Minute Challenge

- Who inspires you?
- Why do they inspire you?
- What can you do to be reminded of that inspiration on a daily basis?

Let's see what **Lucy** and **_Diego_** have written first.

The 5 Minute Challenge – Lucy & Diego

Lucy	Diego
Who inspires you?	
My Lola	Steve Jobs.
Why do they inspire you?	
My lola was my hero, she was so full of joy and love. I want to become more like her.	I love his story of how he grew his company, his comeback and his passion for creation
What can you do to be reminded of their inspiration daily?	
Before she died she gave me one of her favorite necklaces. It is priceless to me. I will display it on my bedroom mirror where I will see it every day	One of my favorite Steve Jobs quotes is 'The only way to do great work is to do what you love' I will print it out and post it on my bedroom wall where I will see it everyday.
How do you feel after doing this exercise?	
This was really powerful for me, I'm too afraid to wear the necklace everyday in case I lose it, but seeing it daily on my mirror will remind me of how much I am loved. Feeling blessed ☺	It is inspiring to read messages like this, still not sure how it will help me with some of the challenges I face. I really do want to do work that I love. Hmm I guess it may help me to not forget this.

To learn how others have completed this exercise – join "The Rise of the Pinoy Community" on Facebook today.

> f The Rise of the Pinoy Community   🔍

The 5 Minute Challenge - Your Turn!

Who inspires you?

Why do they inspire you?

What can you do to be reminded of their inspiration daily?

How do you feel after doing this exercise?

A Note from Mike...

So did you really complete the exercise? Here I go again. I know you may not have expected that I would ask you to do practical exercises like this when you first opened the book but I can't stress enough how important it is for you to do this. One of the biggest mistakes we make when we acquire new information is that we fail to intentionally ask ourselves the question: 'what does this mean to me?' The biggest mistake you could make in reading this book would be to skip these 5 Minute Challenges. Please don't make that mistake. The time to do the 5 Minute Challenge is immediately after you have read the chapter. Let the answers flow from your heart and mind. At the end of the book you will fully understand the extraordinary power of doing this. Thank you again for trusting me on this. We are on this journey together.

CHAPTER 2

Your Unique Assignment

What great achievement would not have happened without you? I want you to really think about it. It could be as simple as the time you led the catering for a child's birthday. Or the time your high school team qualified for the national finals for the first time in its history. Or the time when you and your team worked until 4am to complete the thesis and nailed it. Each one of us, throughout our lives, will be given things to do that were meant for us. However, there will come a time for all of us to be given a very important assignment. A unique assignment that will significantly change your life and the lives of others. An assignment that only you can do.

In April 2010, I got the opportunity to visit Africa as a tourist. I never thought the decision to go would change my life. During the trip, I got a chance to go off the typical tourist trail: I got a chance to visit the African slums. It was the first time I had ever seen people living in extreme poverty. For the first time, I started to question the traditional version of what success means.

It was a massive wake up call about how I was living my life because, if I were honest, up until that point it was all about me. How can Mike be entertained this weekend? How can Mike get more money? How can Mike get the latest gadgets? I never internalized the inequality that the majority of the world suffers from and the role that I played in contributing to that inequality. I made a vow to myself that I would do something.

In the months that followed, I got actively engaged in charities back in the US that were fundraising to promote girls' education in Tanzania and a part of me felt good about myself. However, I reflected back to the promise I made to myself. I asked myself, 'am I really making the biggest possible impact here?' The answer was no. I knew that I needed to return.

> I never internalized the inequality that the majority of the world suffers from and the role that I played in contributing to that inequality

I returned to Tanzania for another two weeks one year later. This time, I spent the majority of my time in a volunteer capacity at a not-for-profit hospital. It was the greatest two weeks of my life. I never felt more alive. The work made my heart sing. However, when the CEO of the hospital made me an offer to work full-time, I got scared. 'Am I really going to do this? Look at everything I would have to give up'. So I did what I thought was the easiest thing and I did not answer his question. I returned to America with my friends welcoming me 'back to reality' but, for me, a fire had been lit inside me that could not be extinguished. I could not allow myself to be crippled by fear. I returned to Africa again the next year, this time for an extended trip of 5 weeks and once again volunteering at this hospital. After just a few days on this trip I knew what my decision must be.

In March 2013, I quit my job in corporate America and moved to Africa. I signed a two year contract to work as the Management and Leadership Coach for this not-for-profit hospital. I was living my unique assignment. Today, it remains one of the best decisions I have made in my life. To my friends and family it looked like I was crazy, but for me it was just the right thing to do. I was so convinced that this was what I must do that I would have rather gone and failed spectacularly than have stayed and never known. That's the power of knowing when you have found your unique assignment. You align yourself with what your inner voice is telling you. Let's now look at the stories of three world-class Filipinos and how they found their unique assignment to live their purpose.

> I was so convinced that this was what I must do that I would have rather have gone and failed spectacularly than to stay and never know

Anna Meloto-Wilk — President, Human Nature

In 2008, Anna, along with her husband Dylan and sister Camille, co-founded Human Nature. Today, Human Nature is the largest homegrown cosmetic and beauty company in the nation employing over 300 people, present in 5 international markets and with a network of 40,000 dealers. Their products are found in every major retail shop with yours truly being a proud daily consumer. When I met Anna (who is also the proud mother of 5 young children), I asked her about the journey that led her to co-create one of the nation's largest social enterprises.

> "Before Human Nature, I was following the typical path most parents would be proud of: I was a graduate from a top university and was employed with one of the biggest broadcasting companies in the country. I did that for 4 years

until one day I came into my office in Makati, I sat down, I turned on my computer and then it just hit me. Anyone can do this job, anyone can come up with these promo plans, anyone can analyze this data. I'm so dispensable here, but I'm really needed somewhere else. That's when I started volunteering for Gawad Kalinga (GK) and using the skills and the experiences that I learned from my corporate life.

It was with GK that I met another volunteer: a young British man called Dylan Wilk. We fell in love and got married. It was in the process of serving others that the idea for Human Nature came about. We didn't know anything about cosmetics, we didn't know anything about how to start a business in the Philippine environment, but we just had this burning desire to do something and the excitement of creation propelled us in the early days. I really believe that, if you take the first step, then the universe will conspire to take you further.

> I really believe that, if you take the first step, then the universe will conspire to take you further

Our generation is always caught up with achieving the American Dream or the Filipino Dream and everything that means. You know, having the two cars, and the house. Everyone's chasing after that. They think it's a dream, but it's really a lifestyle that they want to lead and then, when you reach it, you have to maintain it. But, for me, it's always been about finding a purpose to serve not a lifestyle to lead. It's always a question of 'am I serving a purpose at this moment.' Whether I'm happy about it or not, what is that purpose? That's what makes me happy"

> For me, it's always been about finding a purpose to serve not a lifestyle to lead.

Rey Bufi — Founder, The Storytelling Project

The Storytelling Project is a non-profit organization committed to helping underprivileged Filipino children in remote communities develop the habit of reading and writing. I got the opportunity to meet its founder, Rey Bufi. In the Philippines, Rey observed that reading is primarily regarded as an academic activity, never a pleasurable activity. He and his team wanted to show children that reading is fun and it's not a burden.

Rey explains:

"When I was in elementary and high school, I wasn't a reader. Growing up, my dream was to become a lawyer. When I went to university, I had to read so many articles in a week and then write papers about them. It was a big problem for me. I usually read the articles five times just to understand them. One of my professors advised me to start reading novels that interested me. Then I had this 'light-bulb' moment when I realised that, before, I was reading articles five times, but I was now able to understand them more quickly. So I told myself: "If I only had the chance, when I was a child, to read more books, to have time reading what I wanted, then maybe I would have created this reading habit when I was in college.

I believe that, if we raise a nation of readers, then we will have future citizens who are critical thinkers, who are innovators, who are inventors: full of imagination. That's what storytelling is about: tapping the imagination of the kids. If the kids imagine, there will be so much creation. They can think of

> I believe that, if we raise a nation of readers, then we will have future citizens who are critical thinkers, who are innovators, who are inventors: full of imagination

so many things, they can dream, they can start believing in themselves.

After graduating, I went into the corporate world but this passion for this mission would not go away. So in 2006 I quit my job to focus on pursuing this passion. It was hard. People would tell me, 'Why did you quit your job? And why pursue a career in community development where there is no stable career?' But, as I've said, follow your passion. I had this vision and, for me, if you have that vision in mind, then continue pursuing that vision. There will be a lot of struggles along the way, but you have to focus on that vision. It's always about taking the risk. I know there are a lot of people who will tell you that it can't be done, but it shouldn't be your story about yourself. We have this notion that successful people are those who have stable jobs, stable careers. But for me, it's a different kind of success that I'm looking for and thats in community development, and in empowering the children.

I'm living my vision of creating my own project and every day it amazes me: the opportunities that I'm receiving right now, the people helping our organization. Every day I'm so thankful to have this opportunity to serve, to continue what I'm doing. I will still continue what I'm doing even if there's no other help. I will, because that's my passion, that's who I am. Even if there's no camera involved, it's the same. Even though no one is helping me, I will still give the effort, the passion inside me because that's who I am."

> I know there are a lot of people who will tell you that it can't be done, but it shouldn't be your story about yourself.

Anton Diaz — Founder, Our Awesome Planet

Anton Diaz is one of the most successful online entrepreneurs in the Philippines today. After over 10 years in the industry his food and travel blog 'Our Awesome Planet' has over one million page views every month. Prior to entering blogging full time, Anton was working as a senior executive in one of the largest multinationals in the world. However, he decided to make a change.

"When I quit my job in 2008 people asked me "What will you do now?" I would whisper, 'I'm a blogger', because people don't know what that is or how you're earning. I started blogging about IT and then, on the side, I would blog about the childhood of our kids because I never really knew how I grew up. You have a few photos, and your mother tells you stories, then you get a glimpse of your childhood. What I wanted to do was document the food and travel adventure of our kids, so that when they're old enough they can really read through it. We love to eat. We would blog about our restaurant discoveries. It started as a travel blog going to different beaches and it resonated well with the audience.

You need to have faith. If you don't have that faith then it's very difficult to make it. I always believed that I was touched by the Holy Spirit. I had this vision that I needed to serve those outside of my corporation. I knew that, if I focused on the blog, I'd be able to help a lot of people, and my vision was for a lot people to be hugging me, thanking me for the blog.

> You need to have faith. If you don't have that faith then it's very difficult to make it.

Success for me is getting paid for helping other people, and at the same time getting paid for what you love to do. Before, luxury was all about money. You know, financial independence. I like this quote: 'Luxury is not anymore about just money'. The new definition of luxury is about time and being mobile. This redefined definition means it's luxurious if you can do whatever you want to do, with anybody you want to be with, at any point of time. That continues to inspire me to develop this online business so that I can be location independent. I can spend more time with the family wherever I want to be."

Success for me is getting paid
for helping other people, and at
the same time getting paid for
what you love to do

Powerful Lesson # 2 – You have been given a unique assignment that only you can complete

You have been given a unique assignment in life that you and only you can complete. So how can you find this unique assignment? At different stages of your life, you will be given many unique goals, unique assignments and unique visions. The wisdom comes from being able to differentiate these from your dreams. Dreams are casual fantasies – moments where we escape from the reality of the world. Sometimes these dreams stay with us for a few days, a few weeks or a few years. For example, at different stages of my life, I have dreamed of being a priest, a farmer, a singer, a professional footballer, a vet, a councilor, a politician, a dentist, a chemist and an Irish bar owner. None of these turned out to be my unique assignment.

The worst advice I could give you is to follow your dreams. *Never* follow your dreams. That is so dangerous. Instead, test your dreams. Test them to really find out if this dream is truly a unique assignment given to you and only you. I have coached so many people who have came to me frustrated because they don't have joy in their current job. I tell them that there is good news, because every time you identify something that you are not passionate about or you are not good at, by the process of elimination you take a step closer to finding out your unique assignment. This is good news. The fact that you are even aware you have a unique purpose, when so many are not, is really encouraging news.

Let me now give you your 5 Minute Challenge for this chapter. This is the most creative exercise in the book. Remember every great thing that was ever achieved was first created in the mind. So, the purpose of this exercise is to help you explore your mind like never before. To help you begin the process of identifying your unique assignment. For some of you this exercise will affirm what you already know. For others, new ideas will be created. Everyone will be different. Let's find out yours. Now let your creative juices flow.

The 5 Minute Challenge

- Draw the best version of you 10 years from now?
- Create images the will represent multiple areas of your life, what great thing will you be doing?
- In the picture, capture how amazing you will feel and how blessed others around you will feel?

The 5 Minute Challenge – *Lucy* & *Diego*

Lucy

How do you feel after doing this exercise?
I loved this exercise. It made me come alive. I never really thought of the future like this before. I really want to create my own school one day. I want to be able to give back to my community. I want to be able to provide for my family. I want them to be proud of me.

Diego

How do you feel after doing this exercise?

Wow! I could not believe what I drew. Especially the idea of being a music teacher. My music teacher was such an inspiration for me it would be great to be able to help young musicians develop their talents. It also reminded me that I really want to get in shape. I love playing basketball and I don't want to have to stop. I would also like to be able to give back to the country in some way, like through helping out some music schools in the province, I'm not sure exactly, but it got me excited about the possibilities.

The 5 Minute Challenge - Your Turn!

Draw the Best Version of You – 10 years from now

How do you feel after doing this exercise?

A Note from Mike...

Have you ever said to yourself 'I wish I knew this sooner'? I have. However, an even more powerful regret is 'I wish I did this sooner'. Thank you for acknowledging the importance of application by completing the 5 Minute Challenge for this chapter. The best version of you lies ahead.

CHAPTER 3

Discover Your Motivation

Can you think of a time in your life when you did not quit? When the easiest option would have been to give up or surrender to the pressure of others, but you kept moving forward? For some of you it could be the time you kept studying for that exam despite some of your friends telling you it was a waste of time, or a family member telling you that you were not smart enough. For others, it could be the time they kept looking for a way to help a younger sister complete her homework despite her resistance and lack of concentration. Or perhaps it was that time you kept entering singing competitions despite not winning any trophies for years. The reason why you kept going is your motivation. Knowing your motivation is critical to your success. In everything you do, especially when you look towards the future, you need to know your 'why'.

> In everything you do, especially when you look towards the future, you need to know your 'why'

I look at my family back in Ireland. I am one of four, with two sisters and one brother. My father is a farmer and my mum a care worker. It took me a long time to realize it, but they are the greatest gift I've ever had in life. I had an amazing childhood and couldn't think of a better start to life. My Filipino friends always smile when I show them pictures of our family farm – lots of green and lots of sheep. In

2006, I left Ireland to become what you might call an OIW – Overseas Irish Worker. Since then, I have tried to visit my family at least twice a year. My trips home have always been something that get me really excited. What I noticed in the first few years is that I would treat my siblings the same way as I always did. We laughed together, we made fun of each other and, of course, we fought.

It is normal, right? Siblings are supposed to fight with each other? 'Mum, will you tell him to stop it?' was a classic response that would come from my sister. Then, while I was on the plane home one year to spend Christmas with them, it suddenly hit me: my time with my family was so limited. I would only get to spend two or three weeks a year back in Ireland with them. Did I really want to spend a part of that time in conflict? Did I really want to spend that time arguing over tiny, irrelevant things? Did I really want to spend that time behaving like I was a spoilt teenager again? The answer was a big 'no'. My relationship with my siblings is important to me. It is really important to me, but I was behaving as if nothing had changed from our childhood.

I had to make a change. And that change started with me. Perhaps they did not notice it at first, but I realized that I must model the change that I wanted to see in my own family. I became more kind to them, I became more interested in them, and I became more accepting of them. Showing love to them is always more important than 'being right' and, anyway, a lot of the time I wasn't right. I just wanted to win the argument or the shouting contest. It is so embarrassing to look back at how silly I was. Another big source of inspiration was my Dad, and his relationship with his brother. My Dad is my hero. He has sacrificed so much for my siblings and me. Yet, today, he and his only brother don't talk to each other. I know that this is a cause of massive pain for both of them. I committed myself to never allowing that to happen to my siblings and me. One day, my parents will pass away and my siblings will be the closest connection with my past. I don't want to lose them. I don't want us to become strangers or, even worse, enemies. Discovering my motivation to improve my relationship with my siblings created one of the best changes I have ever made in my life. Let's now look at the stories of four world-class Filipinos about how they discovered their motivation to unleash their potential.

> I realized that I must model the change that I wanted to see in my own family

Ginger Arboleda — Founder, Manila Workshops

Ginger Arboleda is a serial entrepreneur and modern day superwoman. I would run out of space in this chapter if I were to attempt to write about all the different types of businesses that she is involved with. In our interview, I wanted to get a deeper understanding of her motivation to continue to create businesses and, in particular, to help others realize their own entrepreneurial dreams.

"I want my daughter to live in a world where she's safe: where the economy of the Philippines is probably booming; where money is not an issue; where a lot of people, I hope, will be looking to do things they are passionate about that help the Philippines. If people took time to do something that they want, like small things they can do to help the Philippines on a daily basis, we would actually be in a better place as a country.

There were a lot of moments as an entrepreneur where I wanted to quit. But what got me back on track was the bigger, *higher purpose. My goal is to build. In the beginning it wasn't that: it was really to spend more time with my daughter. But then, as the business grew bigger, it was the higher purpose of trying to help people create their own businesses. You really have to start with your 'why' because it's the only thing that you can turn back to or look at during times like this when you don't have support from family or friends.*

We only think about the meaning of life when something bad happens to us or if we find out we have a grave disease or illness. But we don't go through that process of really thinking of what our purpose in life is. When you pass away, you should have something that you have actually done or built: a legacy that you leave behind when you're gone.

You really have to start with your 'why' because it's the only thing that you can turn back to or look at during times like this when you don't have support from family or friends

The real definition of success is getting to that state where you're content and happy with the relationships that you have with your family, with others, with friends. And you just have enough to get you by and to live your dreams. So, I think it's a personal definition. It has to come from the individual.

Success is an emotion that you feel when you know that you've actually done something for yourself or for the community. If we just realize that it's the small things that we can do every day, we can actually make the world a better place."

Steve Benitez — CEO, Bo's Coffee

Steve Benitez is the founder and CEO of Bo's Coffee, the number one homegrown coffee chain in the nation. Steve spoke to me about the power of knowing your motive when you are starting and growing your business.

"When you are about to start a business, people will always say, 'pursue your passion,' 'find your passion,' or 'be passionate about what you're doing'. It's about passion, right?

And people really rush and say, 'Hey! This is what I'm passionate about so I'm going to do this in business.' And then they turn out to be unsuccessful because it actually wasn't their passion, it was just their passion at that particular time. There's a difference – passion is something that you've always wanted to do for the longest time. So, if you're good with cars and you pursue a business in cars, or if you're passionate about clothing, you pursue business in fashion. But if you just want to be in business and say, 'Hey, I just want to be in business, I don't care what kind of business.' that is not passion.

> Don't rush into finding your passion. If you can't find your passion, trust me, your passion will find you

So let's say, for example, that my original passion was traveling. I love to travel, I like to see the world, and I like to see different places. For me, traveling is one of the primary sources of learning: firsthand experience learning about people, learning about culture, or just learning about the place where you are. That's traveling for me. That original passion led me to my next passion, which was coffee, because I enjoyed going to different coffee shops when I traveled to different places.

Don't rush into finding your passion. If you can't find your passion, trust me, your passion will find you.

There was the stage in our growth, going from the tenth to the twentieth store, when I had to really think about whether this thing was for me. One day I said, "Shucks! Do I want to go through this for the rest of my life? Do I want to be an entrepreneur for the rest of my life? Do I want to face all of these challenges first thing in the morning?" Sometimes I couldn't even sleep. So that was the first time I really questioned myself about it. I went through a phase in which I had to really examine myself and I eventually said, 'Yup! I think this is what I want to do for the rest of my life.' I started accepting that, I started accepting, 'Okay, all of these problems are part of being an entrepreneur, I'll embrace it.' I want to be an entrepreneur, these are part of the equation, I said, 'I should start embracing it.' When I started embracing all of these challenges, reaching my goals became easier. Then, from the twentieth to thirtieth stores, I started accepting all of these challenges as part of the journey of an entrepreneur. It got me faster to the fiftieth store. It's about acceptance, accepting where you are, accepting the circumstances - that's the biggest change that I have made in my career."

> When I started embracing all of these challenges, reaching my goals became easier

Marianne Mencias — Best-Selling Author

Marianne Mencias is the best-selling author of "What's your Life Masterpiece" — a book that that aims to unlock the greatness in every Filipino. My interview with Marianne is one my all-time favorites. I asked her about her motivation to write this classic.

"I remember one car-ride back to Manila, I was asking myself, "Why did God make me a Filipino?" and the next question was "Why are there a lot of Filipinos, very successful, very happy with what they are doing, and then at the other end of the spectrum there are people who are so miserable." I don't think that a great life is just for a few. I think it's meant to be experienced by everyone. Then I asked myself "What are these people from that 'happy' part of the spectrum doing right?" So I said, "If I'm going to love the world, love this country the best way I know how to, I'm going to write this book. I'm going to interview the most successful Filipinos and share their wisdom with others. How will I do that? I'm not sure, but that's what's in my heart.

> I don't think that a great life is just for a few. I think it's meant to be experienced by everyone.

Sometimes, I would wake up early in the morning and I wouldn't feel like writing because I wanted to sleep again, and then would I ask myself, 'Why the hell am I doing this? I don't even know if they're going to like my book.' So I typed at the top of my sheet, 'this will help change a lot of lives, this will drive people towards their purpose.' I guess when you're coming from a pure intention of wanting to love, of wanting to contribute, then it's going to manifest and you're going to be surprised with how successful it can become, because your motive is pure. ' Every time you're about to do something, ask yourself 'What is my motive?' This is what I'm trying to practice now. Before I act, before I speak, I take a pause, I pray and ask myself 'What is my motive?' If my motive is driven by love, I go ahead, but if my motive is driven by wanting to please people, then I stop: I don't do it.

A lot of us are driven by 'Oh my gosh, what will people say? ' When I was in high school I was bullied, so that made me a people-pleaser. What would people say, what would people think? But when you have something to share within you that you know will help other people, and when you come to that point of wanting to contribute, then your reputation takes a backseat. When you're writing a book, forget about yourself, and think of your message. Think of how it will help others. Think about dying with peace in your heart because you know you did, what you were supposed to do."

> When you have something to share within you that you know will help other people, and when you come to that point of wanting to contribute, then your reputation takes a backseat

Benjie Abad — Founder, Karinderia ni Mang Urot

Benjie Abad is the founder of Karinderia ni Mang Urot, a soup kitchen that has been providing food for the homeless and street children in Quezon City since 2012. I got the chance to spend time with Benjie, and he told me the story of his motivation to pursue this amazing work.

"When I was walking along Quezon Ave, I saw two kids eating beside the trash bin. I was thinking that the chicken they were eating came from that bin. I thought, if I will give sympathy, that's the end of it. I mean, most people do that when they see something like that: just sympathize without doing anything. For me it's a big injustice to see a Filipino who eats from the trash. So I decided to put up a table every Saturday for the people who get their food from the trash bin and the homeless. At least there would be somewhere they can go to every Saturday where they can eat decent food. It started once a week.

Initially it was my family paying for everything. Then someone told me to post it on Facebook. I was reluctant because I didn't want people to think this is a money-making project. Then I posted it, and my friends and relatives abroad said they would donate cash. I asked them: 'why not create your own soup kitchen instead?' mainly because I didn't want them to think I was using this for money. They said: 'how are we supposed to do that when we're in UAE and Canada and people here don't need it'. So I told them, I would accept it but that I didn't do accounting. I'm responsible to my God. So they sent the money and I had a surplus budget, and I realized it could be done three times a week. So, from then, it happened on Fridays, Saturdays and Sundays. Then I posted it again and some more money came in, so I brought supplies to public schools. Up to now, I have been able to do that for 7 public schools in a span of 3 years.

> People are saying that I'm a hero. I tell them it's not heroism. Feeding the hungry is not heroism. It's reasonable and logical to feed someone in need.

People are saying that I'm a hero. I tell them it's not heroism. Feeding the hungry is not heroism. It's reasonable and logical to feed someone in need. Because, personally, I hate to see people going hungry. So maybe that's my motivation, simple as that. There's no calling or voice in my heart, I just believe that someone hungry needs to be fed. That's how simple my motivation is. What my conscience tells me is that it's all natural to do this. No extra stuff like callings or voices, no. The hungry must be fed. Simple as that.

I pledged to God to do this for the rest of my life. As long as I'm living and breathing, I'm going to do this. That was my pledge and I will honor it. I'm only doing the will of my master. The earth and everything in it is the Lord's. So, there's no need for me to hesitate when someone is in need because we're only stewards of the almighty."

> As long as
> I'm living and
> breathing, I'm
> going to do this.

Powerful Lesson # 3
If your motive is wrong, nothing can be right

The definition of motivation is simple: "your motive for action". It is your big 'why'. It is your specific reason that you go back to when you are tempted to quit, but instead, you keep moving forward. In both business and life we greatly underestimate the power of motivation. We make the assumption that motivation is something that is given to us by someone else. This is a big mistake. True motivation always comes from within. No one can give it to you: everyone must discover it on his or her own.

The great men and women from history are proof of the power of motivation. Some of our heroes were willing to give their own life because they knew without exception their motivation for doing so. Success in life is 80% about knowing your 'why'. If you have the wrong motive nothing can be right. So, let's do a simple experiment to discover your real motivation to improve one particular area of your life.

This 5 Minute Challenge is a very simple pain and pleasure test. The purpose of this is to create your awareness of the consequences of inaction in that area: the consequences of not improving both for yourself and for others that you care about. It also helps you create awareness of the joy of success in this area, of what it would be like for you and others if you significantly improved. It is a powerful exercise. For some, it will give new insights, for others, it will reaffirm what you thought all along. I am convinced that, after completing it, you will have a stronger sense of your own motivation. You will have made big progress.

The 5 Minute Challenge

Select an area in your life in which you are the most determined to make a change. An area in which you feel you need to get to the next level. For example, it could be personal health, a family relationship, your career, your role as a student or as a professional, your spiritual journey, your finances. Once you have identified the area, answer the below questions:

- If I do not improve in this area, what pain will that create for me?
- If I do improve in this area, what pleasure will that create for me?
- If I do not improve in this area, what pain will that create for others?
- If I do improve in this area, what pleasure will that create for others?

Let's see what **Lucy** and **Diego** have written first.

The 5 Minute Challenge – *Lucy* & *Diego*

Lucy – area of focus: career

If I do not improve in this area, what pain will that create for me?	If I do improve in this area, what pleasure will that create for me?
I will be left behind. I will not be able to provide from my daughter. I will be called dumb. I will not be able to pursue my dreams.	I will have more opportunities for my family and myself. I will be able to attract a high paying job. I will be able to choose a career that I want rather than having to take what I am offered

If I do not improve in this area, what pain will that create for others?	If I do improve in this area, what pleasure will that create for others?
I will disappoint my parents. They worked so hard and saved so much to get me into college. It would devastate them. Erika will miss out ☹	My parents will be proud of me, they will see that I am a loyal and faithful daughter; they will be able to retire early because I will be able to provide for them. I will afford to give my daughter the best education possible.

How do you feel after doing this exercise?
This really helped me see my motive. I always knew that it was important to advance my career but this really helped me clarify why – especially the consequences to my family if I don't.

Diego – area of focus: son

If I do not improve in this area, what pain will that create for me?	If I do improve in this area, what pleasure will that create for me?
I will be in constant conflict with my dad. I will not be able to trust him. I would have lost him as a great friend and mentor	I can count on my dad; he can help me with my life. I can count on their support as I go through challenges

If I do not improve in this area, what pain will that create for others?	If I do improve in this area, what pleasure will that create for others?
My mum's heart will break because me and my dad are strangers to each other	My mum and dad are going to be proud of me, overtime they will respect the choices I make to be my own man. They will boast to others of how proud they are

How do you feel after doing this exercise?
I feel emotionally drained after doing this. Haha what a heavy exercise, but it really did help me think, especially of what a great relationship with my parents could look like. This was good

The 5 Minute Challenge - Your Turn!

My area of focus: ....

If I do not improve in this area, what pain will that create for me?	If I do improve in this area, what pleasure will that create for me?

If I do not improve in this area, what pain will that create for others?	If I do improve in this area, what pleasure will that create for others?

How do you feel after doing this exercise?

A Note from Mike...

For a long time, I thought knowledge was power. That is not true. Knowledge without application is useless. Only applied knowledge is power. Thank you for understanding how important this is, by completing the 5 Minute Challenge for this chapter. Being world-class is within your reach.

CHAPTER 4

Your Greatest Enemy

Are you ready for the fight of your life? Sounds scary doesn't it? So you get to the ring and there your opponent stands. The greatest competitor you will ever face. Your most difficult rival. Your most rebellious challenger: you. Yes, that person is you. That negative, disempowering, destructive voice in your head that tells you "I can't do it", "I'm too tired", "I'll do it later", "It's too hard", "I'm too busy", "I have no one to help me", "I have no will power", "I'm not smart enough", "I've failed before", "I'm afraid they will laugh at me".

Do you remember the time you made that New Year's resolution to do the new exercise plan, but you did not even last until February? Or the time you promised your friend that you would go to their party but, when the time came, you were too lazy so instead you pretended that your boss forced you to work overtime in the office? Or the time you promised your mum that you would be nicer to your younger brother but then, less than 48 hours later, you were ignoring him at the dinner table?

I remember these examples very clearly because these are all my personal examples. We all have the same enemy: ourselves. Although there are many examples we could share, I want to share with you one of the greatest personal battles that I have ever had to face.

Earlier in the book, I spoke about one of the biggest decisions I made in my life: to quit my job working for a big multinational in

America to work for a small not-for-profit hospital in Africa. What few people know, including my own family, is the personal struggle that I went through in my first six months in Africa. The truth was that I was going through multiple bad spells of depression in that time period. I did not have a large circle of friends anymore. I did not have the multiple options for distraction anymore. There were times when I was questioning my decision to quit my job. I felt I had made a mistake. I felt very uncomfortable. I felt very lonely.

Then it came to me. Loneliness: is that really the root cause of my pain? Is that really the source of my depression? Am I really that dependent on the approval of others to determine my happiness? I realized that I had misdiagnosed the problem all along. The root cause of my stuggles wasn't loneliness or anything to do with other people. The problem was that I really didn't know myself.

I was significantly out of my comfort zone. My free time was no longer consumed by the noise of TV, video games, parties or sport. There was just silence. I was exposed to allowing the negative voice in my head, feed me the lies that I was powerless, that I was unworthy. I understood for the first time that I never gave myself the opportunity to intentionally explore who I am: to really ask myself the serious questions about where I want to go in life, what I want to achieve, the person I want to become. I did not know what really gave me joy.

> The problem was that I really didn't know myself

I began a process that, to this day, I tell people saved my life. A simple process of journaling: of asking myself important questions and dedicating time to answering them. I began to love the process. I would go to the beach on my own, sit overlooking the water and the words would just flow out of me. I would intentionally schedule "lunch with self" appointments where I would have lunch on my own and, at the same time, journal my thoughts. I never thought that daily journaling would become such a powerful habit for me. The most powerful of these questions was simply asking myself: 'what am I most grateful for right now?'. Taking the time to ask myself that one question every morning had a profound impact on me.

I ended up turning one of the most difficult periods of my life into one of my greatest victories. It all started from recognizing that the battle is always with yourself. It is always within your own mind. Let's now look at the stories of three world-class Filipinos and how they had to overcome themselves first in order to realize their greatness.

> I never thought that daily journaling would become such a powerful habit for me

Tony Meloto — Founder, Gawad Kalinga

Tony Meloto is the founder of Gawad Kalinga (GK), one of the most credible and effective humanitarian organizations operating in the Philippines today. GK has empowered hundreds of thousands of people across Asia to break out of poverty. The work of GK has made international headlines with Tony himself the receiver of many of the awards, praise and media attention.

When I interviewed Tony, I wanted to hear from him about the personal battles he had to fight in order for GK to flourish.

"In the beginning, it was difficult for my wife to see me leave my house at 6 o'clock in the morning and to spend my

Sundays with the gang leaders, with the out-of-school youth, with the drug addicts. It was hard for me to be able to convince my own family that I was doing this for them, because we normally have a very short vision and so we want instant gratification. We live in a world of instant gratification and immediate return on investment but, when you talk about vision, you talk about a future that has to be built now. That will entail a lot of commitment of time and talent, and families saying, 'Hey! That should come to us because charity begins at home,' so you're actually challenging traditional thinking and that's what disruption is about. So, when I spend time with the gang leaders, my family also gets concerned, 'They're dangerous. Why are you spending time with them? We are your family. Why don't you just spend more time earning more money so that you can give us a better quality of life?'

> It was hard for me to be able to convince my own family that I was doing this for them

But sacrifice builds character. No nation is built without sacrifice, no social enterprise is built without sacrifice, and no family is built without sacrifice. If you treat humanity as family then every ounce of sacrifice is used to make the world better, to build humanity. You use all your knowledge, every technology, every resource at the service of greater humanity.

Today I struggle the most with glory. Because the world is always looking for a rock star. I have difficulty with all the media attention. I'm here just as a storyteller to let the world know that there are extraordinary people in the world, being recognized as a trustworthy spokesperson for the weak and the powerless, or the strong who are helping the weak... that somehow draws

> Sacrifice builds character. No nation is built without sacrifice, no social enterprise is built without sacrifice, and no family is built without sacrifice.

a lot of support to ease human suffering. However, it's never been about me, and I struggle a lot when I'm on the global stage, because the work of GK is the work of millions. I'm happy to be the face, but they want to attribute superhuman powers to you.

Recently, I was at a global forum where they called me a leader from Asia changing the world. When you get a standing ovation from thousands of people, you have a choice to bask in the glory or to go back to what it is all about. I went back home, went back to the farmers, went back to the informal settlers, because I wouldn't be on that stage if not for them. It's not about me: it's about the greatness of the human spirit that is in everyone."

Rebecca Bustamante — President, Asia CEO Forum

Rebecca Bustamante is the President of the Asia CEO Forum and is considered one of the most accomplished female entrepreneurs working in the Philippines today. She spent 15 years as an OFW in Singapore and Canada before deciding to return home. She shared with me the battles that occurred within her own mind.

"There were five children in my family and I was the oldest. When I left the Philippines, I was 19 years old and my youngest brother was only 6 years old. That was painful, that was hard. My father was always drunk and had no proper job, so I wondered who would be looking after them. We didn't have a mother and, going to Singapore, I didn't know anybody. It was my first time to go abroad, and I had never been on an airplane before. That was tough, that

was so lonely. As soon as I arrived in Singapore, I started to miss my family so much. Every time I spoke to them they were always asking for money because they needed money, so that creates more loneliness, right? I didn't have days off. I had one day off a month but then I could not go out because I used that day off to pursue my education.

So how did I handle that? I focused on what I could do to go to the next level in my career. So instead of crying, thinking about that, I focused on how to be better; how to be better for my family; how to go to the next level of my career. That's how I overcame my loneliness.

> So instead of crying, thinking about that, I focused on how to be better; how to be better for my family; how to go to the next level of my career.

I had the opportunity to work in Singapore as a domestic helper, and I was proud to be a domestic helper: that was a stepping stone to go to the next level in my life in order to help my family back home. When I was in Singapore, I had the opportunity to pursue my education and at the same time read a lot of books. When I went to Canada I pursued my education again and I also did a lot of learning, attending a lot of seminars, trainings. Not only did I learn to develop myself, but also how to connect with the right people, learning from their experiences, how to be like them, what I needed to do in order to secure my success. So that's what I did.

I've gone through so many setbacks because when you're young you don't have self confidence. People call you names. How do you handle that? People laugh at you. I said 'It's okay, because I know where I'm going. I have a vision, I have goals.' You make sure that you're always in charge of your life. You control your mind, your feelings, and your emotions. Don't let emotions control you. It is so important to really manage yourself, manage your mind, and not let your mind manage you."

> You make sure that you're always in charge of your life. You control your mind, your feelings, and your emotions. Don't let emotions control you.

Boris Joaquin — CEO, Salt and Light Ventures

Boris is one of the most successful leadership speakers and trainers in the Philippines today. I got the pleasure of seeing Boris in action and was really impressed by his ability to connect with the audience. Looking back over his career, he spoke to me about overcoming the battle of self.

"Like every leader I have a major ego problem. It's probably a combination of pride and fear. In my case, it's really being more self-centered. I think we're naturally self-centered in so many ways. When ego becomes the focus of my leadership and the things that I do, I normally fail. A lot of things crumble because it clouds your vision. Because normally, your vision, if it's noble, goes beyond yourself. I think the failures I had in life, whether running a business that went bankrupt or whether in a career that went south, were because I had been infected with my ego virus called pride. I allowed that to creep into my mind.

Everyone experiences fear. I tend to be fearful of things,

like somebody might belittle my leadership or somebody might try to dethrone me, if I am even sitting on a throne. That fear engulfs my being to build a self-protective defense mechanism. So you build this wall and you're building a wall against nothing because there's really nothing there. Fear is not real. Fear is false evidence appearing real. I'm not saying that I've completely overcome it. It's still an on-going battle.

> When ego becomes the focus of my leadership and the things that I do, I normally fail

When good and bad collide, who do you think would win?' 'Whoever you feed the most.' So, if you feed your pride and fear more, it probably grows into a monster. Failure wins because we feed it, and it devours the very people who are closest to us first because they're immediately there. The monster comes out on top. The moment that you get infected with pride in thinking that you're better than anybody is the first day of your downfall because you probably won't be willing to listen to anything else.

My advice to a lot of leaders out there: is when you feel things are not going well, then journal. That is the therapeutic action that has really helped me overcome my fears and be a more effective leader. I think that's good advice to a lot of leaders out there."

> Failure wins because we feed it

Powerful Lesson # 4

The quality of the questions you ask yourself will determine your destiny

The greatest fight you will ever face is against yourself. This is the same for me, all of our world-class Filipinos, and it is the same for you. You must not allow yourself to become a victim of negative thinking. The key difference between winners and losers in life is the questions they ask themselves. Losers always look towards lack of resources (time, money, contacts) as the reason they are not achieving their goals. They say things like "Why is this happening to me?" "Why won't someone do something?" "When will someone fix this?". When winners are struggling to achieve their goals they always look within. Their focus is on becoming more resourceful. They ask questions like "What could I have done differently?" "What can I learn from this?" "What can I do to improve this situation?". You change your question. You change your life. This is why the battle of the mind is so important on the journey to becoming world-class.

Let me now give you your 5 Minute Challenge for this chapter. This could be the most satisfying exercise in the book. In this exercise I will ask you to recognize yourself for what you have already achieved. To acknowledge yourself for the good person you are today. To appreciate yourself for the commitment you are making to becoming a better version of you. Remember you have already won many victories against yourself. You would not even be reading this book right now if you did not have amazing successes in the battle against yourself.

The purpose of this exercise is to build on your existing successes. The downfall of too many people is they constantly focus on what's not going well, areas of their life where they are falling short or negative behaviors in their life that's causing them massive pain. They forget to see the positives and thus fail to build on them. I don't want you to make this mistake. You are an amazing person. You are a wonderful person. You are greatly loved. I am proud of you for reading this book. Now this is your time to remember and recognize the goodness that is already within you.

The 5 Minute Challenge

What do you want to recognize and acknowledge yourself for? For example

- Something that you have achieved in the past that you are proud of?
- A time that you have said 'no' and that you are really glad you did?
- A situation where others saw the best of you?

Let's see what **Lucy** and *Diego* have written first.

The 5 Minute Challenge – *Lucy* & *Diego*

Lucy

> **I want to recognize and acknowledge myself for...**
>
> Being a good mother. For asking my friends advice on how I can become a better mum as she really helped me. For being single and waiting for the right guy. For caring so much for my family. For being a good daughter, I really do try to help my mum at home and I know I make Papa really proud. I really do love my siblings. For being faithful to God. I know He has great plans for me. For believing that I am special. For believing that I can become world-class one day.

> **How do you feel after doing this exercise?**
>
> Oh I'm feeling so proud of myself. Sometimes I feel down when I see others having so much more than me, but this really helped remind me that I have come a long way. I am a good person and I know I can win the fight – against my self

Diego

> **I want to recognize and acknowledge myself for...**
>
> *Being a good friend. I am always there for my friends when they need me. I am a good guy and they know that they can trust me. For being a dedicated student of music, I am really proud that I kept my practice routine up and I am constantly looking to improve. For wanting a better relationship with my Dad. The easiest thing to do would be to do nothing, but I am glad I am aware and have this strong desire to improve it. For reading this book – haha – I can't believe I have made it this far ;-P*

> **How do you feel after doing this exercise?**
>
> *I have to admit I am feeling pretty empowered after that exercise. I am a good man, my friends are proof of that. Yes I like this.*

The 5 Minute Challenge - Your Turn!

> **I want to recognize and acknowledge myself for...**

How do you feel after doing this exercise?

A Note from Mike...

> I want to acknowledge you for completing this 5 Minute Challenge. You have done a great thing today. You have started to change your own belief system. As your belief system is the foundation to your success, you have really made a big leap on your journey. I am proud of you. Now let us keep moving forward together on this journey.

CHAPTER 5

Embrace Your Pain

Why do bad things happen to good people? It is the most difficult question that one can ever try to answer. But I know that there is no way you can write a book about realizing your greatness, unleashing your potential, and becoming world-class without talking about adversity. Adversity is what others will call "times of difficulty and hardship". We are all affected by adversity. The type and duration of that adversity will be different for everyone. For some of us it is not getting that job or passing that exam, even though we worked so hard to get to that point. For others it is the pain of a broken family relationship: of someone you thought would be there to support you but who has instead given you discouragement when you needed them the most. For others, it's the feeling that they are surrounded by lack of opportunities: that, no matter how hard they try, they'll never get a break, and will never have the abundant life they deserve.

> We are all affected by adversity. The type and duration of that adversity will be different for everyone

This is the hardest chapter of the book. There is a reason for adversity. There is a purpose to pain. For many of you, this will be the hardest thing to accept in this book. It will take you enormous courage to complete the 5 Minute Challenge at the end of this chapter. But it is necessary. Holding onto anger, holding onto this pain is like drinking poison and expecting someone else to die. It will eventually destroy you. It will hold you back from completing your unique assignment. It will hold you back from your purpose. It will hold you back from becoming world-class. I know this will not be easy but, together, we can do this.

So let me go first. I will share with you my greatest pain: being rejected by my first love. Man tear. I think all the men reading this will agree that the most painful thing in the world is when the girl you love breaks your heart.

For a long time I wondered if I should share this story or not. Then I realized that, if I were to be of greatest service to you, then I must lead by example. I must be willing to share with you my greatest hurt. So here it is.

It was 2008 and I was living in England. I had been dating Katey for a year and I was on top of the world. She was my first real girlfriend and the first girl I had ever fallen in love with. I was already dreaming about marriage and kids. And then (what for me was out of the blue) she told me she didn't love me anymore and she wanted to see other people. To say I was devastated was an understatement. I did not understand what was happening. I desperately tried to get her back, from emotional love letters to asking friends to speak with her, to begging God to change her mind. But she did not. Those six months after she said those words was one of the toughest periods of my life. I really struggled to accept that I had been dumped.

In my attempt to "move on" I decided to bury her memory deep in my mind. The truth was that it took me years to heal this wound.

> Holding onto anger, holding onto this pain is like drinking poison and expecting someone else to die

I never realized that this hurt would show up five years later when I was going through spells of deep depression. I finally had the courage to speak to a professional counselor in the hope that they would be able to help me. In my conscious mind, I had already forgotten about Katey: I had moved on; I had deleted that file from my desktop. When the councilor asked me about my greatest pain I experienced in my life, I mentioned her name, but then quickly tried to change the conversation to something else. I mean: that break-up happened years ago. Why would it impact me today? The truth was that it was significantly impacting me. It then became clear to me that if I did not heal this hurt it would significantly negatively impact my future: especially a future relationship and a family of my own.

> It then became clear to me that if I did not heal this hurt it would significantly negatively impact my future

How I healed the wound was very simple. The counselor asked me if I had photos of us together. I told her that I still had photos somewhere, but that I had not looked at them for years. I was even afraid to search her name on Facebook. I thought it would be too painful. The counselor gave me a homework assignment. She told me to get the photos from my archive and, when I saw the pictures of us together, to think of the happy times we had together. Think of the joy we brought to each other's lives. That was a game changing moment for me.

For the first time, I realized that how I was looking at the situation was the problem all along. I was focusing on the wrong thing. I realized that, when I thought of her name, I only focused on the pain... like the night she broke up with me, or my desperate attempts to win her back. I forgot about all the great times we had. We were each other's first love. No one can take that experience away from us. 95% of our time together was amazing: we made each other laugh so much. I realize I had been looking at my past from a sense of scarcity: that something irreplaceable had been taken away from me. The truth is that our relationship made me a better man, it prepared me for my future. Not only did it help me to be a great husband and father one day, it also "qualified" me to help people who have also gone through this pain. So, amazing as it may sound, I am grateful to her. I am grateful for our relationship, including the breakup. It has made me a better person. It took me five years, but I healed that wound. I am no longer holding onto the pain. It took a lot of courage but I am really glad I took the advice of my friends and sought the help of others. Let's now look at the stories of four world-class Filipinos and how they were able to embrace their pain to achieve outstanding success.

Noey Lopez — CEO, Starbucks Philippines

Noey Lopez is the man who brought Starbucks to the Philippines. Since 1996, he has led the organization, as its CEO, to be one of the most successful and admired franchises in the country. Some of the largest multinational companies in the country come to Noey and his team to learn about how they empower their people to deliver such great customer service at the 200+ stores located across the nation. What most people don't know about Noey is his personal journey to overcome adversity in leading a business early in his career before leading Starbucks.

"I failed miserably. I wasn't able to turn that business around. However I don't think Starbucks in the Philippines would be where it is today if I hadn't gone through that. Or I wouldn't be where I am today if I hadn't gone through that. It was a huge failure but again it taught me so much. Failing miserably taught me where to look. In business, you cannot look at everything: too many moving parts. There are just a

few places where you need to look if your business is healthy, and the experience taught me that.

> It was a huge failure but again it taught me so much. Failing miserably taught me where to look.

I remember in the early years, when we were starting Starbucks, I would say 'no' to a vacation because I was building the company from the ground up. I was working 15-16 hours a day. Some of my family members were distraught, but I think if somebody gives you responsibility, you take it seriously: you know what to do.

What excites me and what drives me is to prove, not just to the world but to ourselves, the Filipino community, that we can be world-class. My goal is to build a company that will show the Filipino excelling. I wanted to use Starbucks as a vehicle to do that and make Filipinos proud. I never thought that I could lead a company like Starbucks in the Philippines. I never thought I had the confidence to do it. But there is no substitute for hard work. You can work smart but you also have to work hard. There's no shortcut. There are so many reasons to give up. I think giving up always haunts you. Right? It'll last forever. I would never call myself academic or intellectual, but I am where I am today by never giving up. What I have seen in 18 years of running Starbucks in the Philippines is that the most successful people are the ones who never give up."

> My goal is to build a company that will show the Filipino excelling. I wanted to use Starbucks as a vehicle to do that and make Filipinos proud.

Pocholo Gonzales — CEO, Creative Voices

Pocholo Gonzales is the CEO of Creative Voices, and one of the most sought - after motivational speakers in the country. He is a veteran voice artist, a radio broadcaster and known to hundreds of thousands of people around the world as the "VoiceMaster of the Philippines". His ability to use his voice to entertain, inspire and empower others never fails to amaze me. In my interview with Pocholo, I asked him about the role adversity has had on shaping his success.

"I grew up in a not so well-off family. We were living in a very small house, the house of my grandmother. We had this very small room for our family. That's when I started dreaming. When I was 10 years old, my first dream was to have my own ball, then my own bike and, finally, my own computer. That Christmas, I wrote a note to Santa and said, "Dear Santa, please give me a ball, a bike and a computer." I put it on our roof, believing that Santa would read it. The next morning, I saw my paper and there was no ball, no bike, no computer. That made me believe that there's no such thing as Santa Claus. Right there and then, I realized the only person that can make dreams a reality is yourself.

> I realized the only person that can make dreams a reality is yourself

During my first year in college, I had the chance to work and the first things I bought were a ball, a bike and a computer. I discovered that I am my own Santa Claus. Everything that we have in life must come from your own hard work. The world will discourage you to do what you love because others do not follow their dreams. I mean, 90% of the people around you are frustrated people, bitter people: a lot of them die with regrets. That means people around you don't want you to be happy because they're not happy: that's the reality. Even your own parents, sometimes. If you follow what your heart desires then you will never be wrong.

I focus more on the strengths, rather than the weaknesses. I make myself do things that I'm good at and forget those things that I'm not good at. When I was in college, I recognized my weakness was in mathematics. Anything that you're not good at is a roadblock. If you ask some people what they are going to do with their weaknesses, they say, "I will work on my weaknesses", and that's the most stupid thing you will ever hear. Why? Why would you work on your weaknesses if you can work on your strengths more? If you work on your weaknesses, you become average but if you work on your strengths, you become the best at what you do."

> If you work on your weaknesses, you become average but if you work on your strengths, you become the best at what you do.

Vince Golangco — Founder, When in Manila

Vince Golangco is the founder and publisher of "When in Manila": the nation's go-to online lifestyle magazine. With over 10 million impressions per day, the online platform that Vince has created is extraordinary. I sat down with Vince to reflect on the impact adversity has had on his personal growth. He spoke to me about a moment earlier in his career that was a painful setback.

"I remember one of my biggest events as a host and I was so nervous. It was one of my first events. The organizers knew me, and they believed in me, so they took a risk on me. At the same time, my talent fee was really low so that was probably also a factor in why they got me. It was a really big event. And the only thing was I know I was pretty bad. There were even some people at the event tweeting about how bad I was.

> I don't see problems as setbacks as long as you learn from them.

Looking back, I understand the importance of not letting it get to you personally. Use the negative experience as a kind of chip on your shoulder to get better. I think that really pushed me to try to be better. It was one of my biggest events and I still remember that there were quite a lot of people who said: 'He's no good'. I think using that as a motivation to do better and to learn from it really helped me out. I don't see problems as setbacks as long as you learn from them. I feel like you gain something. I appreciate setbacks and failures because you learn from them. You have to use adversity in a positive way by letting the pain drive you to do better. Find a way to use it: find a way to use the pain.

Throughout my career there have been a couple of times I was close to quitting. What stopped me from doing so was just remembering that, if you quit, it's forever. But if you live through the pain of the moment, you start to get over it. Find your inner strength for those 2 seconds, for that day, that week, whatever it might be. After that, you gain strength whereas, if you quit, you just stop forever.

You can even take a break but don't completely stop. Take a break from that situation and then come back. But don't completely quit. Because, believe it or not, there are probably a lot of people who have gone through the same stuff you've gone through. But the people who don't quit end up stronger."

Issa Cuevas-Santos — Director, Gawad Kalinga

One of the most remarkable stories in this entire book is that of Issa Cuevas-Santos. Issa is one of the leaders of Gawad Kalinga, the humanitarian organization that is leading millions of people out of poverty across the Philippines. I sat down with Issa as she shared her story.

"I grew up in the province, with a family relatively blessed compared to others. I always thought that's the very best security blanket. I lived my life thinking I was very safe and that I would have a very happy family. I never really thought that my father would be assassinated when I was 13 years old. When you have violence committed against you, it creates an anger inside of you that can really be a chip on your shoulder. And if you really have that kind of anger with you for the rest of your life, the world becomes a very unpleasant place.

My father was killed by a communist rebel, not for personal reasons. In fact I have come to understand that he had nothing against my father, and I realize today that no person in their right mind would choose to be a killer. So, killers exist because we live in a world today where there are no other options. And so, to me, it became not an issue of forgiveness towards him, but really forgiveness towards the system in which we live today, I wasn't the only victim: he was one, too. That is the single most

> That is the single most powerful thing I have learned, that forgiveness is often just thinking less of yourself and putting yourself in the other person's shoes

powerful thing I have learned, that forgiveness is often just thinking less of yourself and putting yourself in the other person's shoes.

I don't think we ever willingly want to do something evil towards one another. At least, to me, it is clear that he was more of a victim than I was. I think I was just the secondary victim to a greater crime that was committed, in which he was forced to participate. He was probably in poverty. If he had a choice in the matter, he would have not chosen to kill my father, So my mission has always been to create a world where people don't have to make that choice – where they can choose to be what they want to be.

I think the best change I have ever made in my life has been just to face life every day with courage and hope. There was a point in my life where it wasn't like that, I think. There really were many years when I couldn't wake up with that hope, and I think it's easier to succumb to hopelessness, to despair. Even when I did figure out that I could change my life, it took a lot of courage because it's a lot easier to stay in a comfort zone where you're sad, or you're depressed, or your angry, or you're thinking about yourself. It really takes courage, not one time courage, but every day courage, to wake up and say, 'I have a chance to shape my life the way I think it should be.' I have a chance to go after my purpose and that takes a lot of courage. It still takes a lot of courage today."

The best change I have ever made in my life has been just to face life every day with courage and hope

Powerful Lesson # 5

Embracing your pain qualifies you to be of greater service to a greater number of people

Overcoming adversity is a requirement for success. It cannot be avoided. I can't tell you how much I wish that this was not true. How I wish for an easier path for both you and me. But that is not realistic. We must face the brutal truth. Every adversity has a purpose. My strong belief is that adversity exists not to break you, not to crush you, not to defeat you. The purpose of adversity is to make you stronger, to make you wiser, to make you more courageous. When you overcome your adversity, when you embrace your pain, you are now qualified to be of greater service to a greater number of people. Think about it. That's a wonderful thought. How can you help someone heal from a broken heart if you never have had your own heart broken? It is a difficult truth for us to accept but it is still a truth. Embracing this truth will set us free. Embracing our pain will set us free.

Perhaps the most painful part of adversity, especially if you are the victim, is not only forgiving those who have done you wrong but to be proactive and begin your own healing process. I am calling on you to identify your pain and take the first step. I do not want you to wait for someone else to make the first move. If ever there is a moment of courage needed in this book, this is it. You have the power within you to convert the most painful moments in your life into the trigger to start the greatest transformation of your life. The transformation of you. I know you have the power in you to do this. I believe in you.

Now: your 5 Minute Challenge for this chapter. This is the toughest exercise in the book. So maybe your first test will be to forgive me for giving you such a heavy challenge. But I give you this exercise for a reason. Every person must go through adversity. However, it is those who use this adversity to become even stronger, to become better, whom achieve greatness in life. The purpose of this exercise is to help you to begin the process of healing a hurt in your life. This process will first ask you to make peace with yourself. I ask you to only pick a wound that you are ready to heal, as there are many hurts you may have for which now is not the right healing time. I understand that. But for sure there is a hurt you are ready to heal. It is time to begin the process.

The 5 Minute Challenge

- Identify a pain in your life that you are ready to heal
- Acknowledge the pain this has caused you
- Forgive those involved for their shortcomings
- Acknowledge that you, too, need to ask for their forgiveness
- Identify what the next action for you is in the healing process

Let's see what **Lucy** and *Diego* have written first.

The 5 Minute Challenge – *Lucy* & *Diego*

Lucy

What pain in your life are you ready to heal?
One of my best friends Grace (we had a big fight last month and we have not spoken since)

Tell them how much pain this has caused you?
You don't know how much you hurt me Grace. I trusted you so much. I told you things that I didn't tell anyone. I thought we would be best friends forever. I feel so betrayed by you.

Tell them that you forgive them.
I forgive you Grace, you probably don't know how much your words hurt me when we had that fight. You were more than just a friend you were like a sister to me. I know you are going through a lot of pressure at work. I know that deep down you are really a good person.

Ask them to forgive you.
I think it is not fair for me to blame you entirely for the break down of our friendship. I know I was not the best of listeners, when you needed me the most, I know I did not give you the best of me. I did not show you enough about how much I care about you. I want you to forgive me Grace for not expressing my friendship better. I am really sorry.

> **What is the next action for you to heal this pain?**
>
> *I don't need to hold on to these bad feelings. When I think of Grace I will repeat to myself "I'm sorry, I love you, forgive me". I will make the first move. I will send her a text message that will make her smile when she reads it. I want her to know that I still care about her*

> **How do you feel after doing this exercise?**
>
> *This made me cry. I feel so hurt. I don't like having these bad feelings towards Grace. I feel so relieved after doing this – it is like there is a big weight released from my shoulders*

Diego

> **What pain in your life are you ready to heal?**
>
> *My Dad (putting me under pressure to join the family business and stop wasting my time with my guitar)*

> **Tell them how much pain this has caused you?**
>
> *You have hurt me Dad. I really want you to support my choice of career. You make me feel stupid when you make fun of my music. This is more than just a hobby, Dad: it is my passion. I wish you would stop putting so much pressure on me to follow in your footsteps. I love you Dad but I am a different person from you.*

> **Tell them that you forgive them.**
>
> *I forgive you Dad. I know deep down you want the best for me, I guess you also followed your father's footsteps so it is only natural that you think that this is what you should tell me. I know you are not a fan of music so I forgive you for not understanding how beautiful an art form it is.*

> **Ask them to forgive you.**
>
> *I have to accept that I am not a total victim here. I have not been really good at expressing myself to you Dad. I really have never told you how unhappy I am being an engineer, I never even told mum. I ask for your forgiveness for not being able to communicate to you better.*

What is the next action for you to heal this pain?

I want to make you proud Dad, but I know I must be free. I'm afraid to talk to you about it as we have never had these types of conversations before. First I will talk to mum about how I feel, as she knows Dad more than anyone, perhaps she can advise me on how we can improve our relationship... or maybe I will just ask her – how can I be a better son?

How do you feel after doing this exercise?

This is so tiring man ... this was a hard chapter. I was surprised that I was able to do this. At the beginning I thought that this is too dramatic but at the end I came out with a good reflection.

I was very skeptical that I must take responsibility. I did not like that. However, after going through the exercise, I learned something important about myself. I have made big progress.

The 5 Minute Challenge - Your Turn!

What pain in your life are you ready to heal?

Tell them how much pain this has caused you?

Tell them that you forgive them.

Ask them to forgive you.

What is the next action for you to heal this pain?

How do you feel after doing this exercise?

A Note from Mike...

> Thank you! Thank you so much for doing this. It breaks my heart to see you in pain. You are so special to this world, if I were beside you right now I would give you a big hug. I want to encourage you to share what you have learned from this experience with someone that you care about. Remember: **everyone is fighting a hard battle**. Because of your courage you may inspire them to begin their unique process of healing. You have done a great thing today. Now rest. You have passed the halfway point of the book. Tomorrow we will start a new chapter. I can't wait for the world to see the world-class person you are becoming. I am so proud of you.

Your story matters

I want you to remember that your story matters. There will be always someone out there, who will benefit from you sharing your experiences. "The Rise of the Pinoy" Facebook Community, exists for that very reason.

> **f** | The Rise of the Pinoy Community

If you haven't done so already, join the community. I want to encourage you to use this platform to share your reflections from doing the exercises in this book.

CHAPTER 6

Your Daily Victory

Can a small change really make a difference? What if the impact of your change is so small you can't even measure it? What's the point of even making a change if you can't feel the effect straight away?

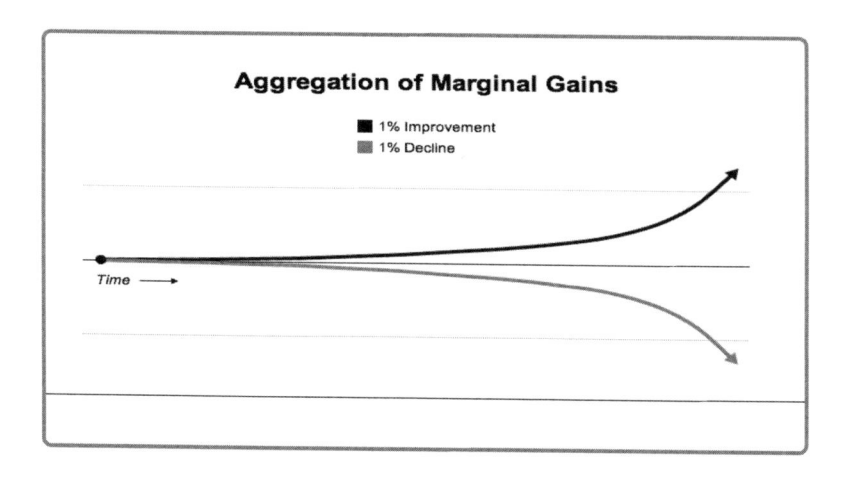

Aggregation of Marginal Gains
- 1% Improvement
- 1% Decline

Time →

This chapter is here to tell you that the small things do matter. For, if you consistently repeat small practices over time, you will create a transformational impact that you can not only measure and feel, but also that will create such a transformational impact that others will stand up and say, "Hey what has happened to you? You have changed!"

Let's take a few examples: Think about when you were learning a new language - You did not just attend one class and become fluent over night, It was a process that took time. Just one new word a day until, eventually, you could put a few sentences together. Think of one of your oldest friendships. You didn't become best friends after just one dinner together. Your friendship blossomed because of the accumulation of the little things: those small acts of kindness you did over the years that created so much trust between you. Or think of a baby learning to walk. The baby did not just say one day 'ok now it's time to walk, and start dancing around the house.' It was a gradual process of crawling then falling, standing then falling, moving forward then falling until eventually that baby couldn't stop dancing. The small things really do matter in life.

> If you consistently repeat small practices over time, you will create a transformational impact

I was recently interviewed on the topic of personal change. The reporter asked me one of the best questions I have ever been asked: "What is the best small change you have ever made in your life?" I love this question. For most of my adult life, I always considered myself "reasonably healthy". Today, looking back, I am embarrassed about how ignorant I was. I was treating my body terribly. That was evident on a daily basis. For years, I struggled with bad skin, being overweight, frequent heartburn and late-afternoon energy crashes. Worst of all, I just accepted this as a part of life. I never realized that what I was drinking and eating was causing this pain all along.

As I write this, I am in the best shape of my life: ideal weight, clear skin, abundant energy, and no more heartburn. I never realized that this was possible for me. I have totally transformed my health. People I know who have not seen me for a while often comment on my physical appearance. I share this with you not to impress you but to express a very important point. Making tiny changes in how I eat has completely transformed my health. It took me less than 30 days to transform my body. Actually, after just a few days, I could feel the power of the change. I don't claim to be an expert in the field of nutrition but I can speak with total confidence on the change that has happened to me.

> Making tiny changes in how I eat has completely transformed my health

So let me share with you my answer to that reporter's question. My response was "my breakfast". Before I began my health transformation, toasted bread and breakfast cereal was what I ate for almost every breakfast of my life for as long as I can remember. I thought it was a healthy choice but I was wrong. When I finally decided that I wanted to take my health to the next level, I asked my friend Marc Daubenbuechel if he could recommend someone to me. The first person he said was Chad Davis. I did not know it then, but Chad is the Philippines' number one health and wellness coach. The guy is a nutrition genius. He looked at my breakfast and informed me how poor of a decision I was making. His advice was simple: switch to eggs and homemade blended green juice (kangkong + banana + honey + water). The change, although so tiny, had a huge impact on me. I believe it was one of the key changes I made that resulted in my health being transformed. It's the power of the tiny change. It's the power of the daily victory. Let's now look at the stories of four world-class Filipinos to discover what daily victories they have mastered in order to achieve their goals.

David Bonifacio — Executive, CBTL Holdings

David Bonifacio is an executive at CBTL holdings where he is the Managing Director of New Leaf Ventures and CEO of Bridge Southeast Asia. David is possibly one of the wisest people I have met since I moved to the Philippines. Outside of business, he is a passionate writer and one of my favorite bloggers. His writings have been a constant source of inspiration to me. During our interview, David and I talked about the habit of reading.

"The first thing I would recommend is to learn how to read the way I did. My parents told me that "There's no one who became really great without reading or learning a massive amount of information." The reason is that "you can only achieve what you believe is within the realm of possibility." For example: the Wright Brothers. They believed they could fly, they really believed it, so they were able to work towards achieving it. No one will ever achieve anything that's beyond the realm of possibility from an intellectual or imagination level.

> There's no one who became really great without reading or learning a massive amount of information

When I was a kid, I wasn't a reader and so I forced myself to read one page every day. I needed to learn how to read yet I hated reading, so I read one page a day. Forcing myself, that one page became two pages, three pages, four pages, then it became one chapter. That one chapter became one chapter from multiple books. The thing I would tell people is to first work on that discipline of learning to read one page. Force yourself. What you're learning is not just the information from the book but the discipline of reading. Then start forcing yourself towards more than one page, two pages, three pages and then one chapter, and then move forward from there. That's how I would approach it.

> What you're learning is not just the information from the book but the discipline of reading

When I was first starting in business, I read a lot of 'For Dummies' books. Subject matter books. For example, I would try to raise funds and then someone would say "Your accounting sucks.", so I'd buy Accounting for Dummies. Or I'd look at Wikipedia, Google, anything I could find on Accounting, and start reading it. *One thing that really helped me was hitting a wall and then saying "Okay, what can I read to break through this wall?" I know I need it, so I just might as well read it."*

Marv De Leon — Founder, Freelance Blend

Marv De Leon is the founder of the Freelance Blend, a community that champions the Filipino freelancer. His vision is to eliminate unemployment in the Philippines through freelancing. Let me start by saying that you may not be even reading this book today without Marv. I attended one of Marv's workshops when I first moved to the Philippines. He was the one who convinced me to start my own podcast, which enabled me to interview all the world-class Filipinos featured in this book. He is one of the mentors that really helped me realize how I could best serve the Philippines. In one of our meetings, we were discussing the importance of having a morning routine. I shared with him some of the habits that I do every morning and I was amazed when he shared with me weeks later that he, too, began to build these new daily victories into his morning.

"The first thing that I do when I wake up is my exercise, apart from Sundays when I take a break. I walk around my village for 30 minutes and I take my iPhone and earphone with me to listen to a podcast that I follow. So, while I'm exercising I am listening to something inspiring and empowering. It really helps me. I found it addictive, because sometimes when you wake up you feel very sluggish and you look for coffee just to wake you up. Well, I still take coffee but I've found it more energizing to do my morning walks and listen to a podcast. I really try to learn something new every day, so that's what the podcasts give me. When I come back from my walk, I take my breakfast and, after that, I do some journaling. For

> While I'm exercising I am listening to something inspiring and empowering

> Whenever I'm down, I read those emails and feedback from people who really value what you give them

example, if there is something from the podcast that I just listened to that I need to remember, then I write it down. After writing, I meditate for a period of time: typically, I listen to a guided mediation from YouTube. My last step is visualization, when I look at my vision board, which includes all the major things that I want to achieve in life. Just a few weeks into starting this morning routine, it has already changed my life.

It's a rollercoaster ride, being a freelancer: sometimes you're up, sometimes you're down. These morning habits really help set my day up for success. Another habit that has been really powerful for me is keeping a file and folder of all the positive feedback I receive. I don't get lots and lots of feedback, but the simple 'thank you's' from a listener or a reader, telling me how I helped them with their problem: that really means a lot to me. So, whenever I'm down, I read those emails and feedback from people who really value what you give them."

Lloyd Luna – Motivational Speaker

Lloyd Luna, popularly known in social media as #PambansangInspirasyon, is an international motivational speaker, popular comedian and the author of eleven self-help books. For such a young man, he has achieved extraordinary success on stage as a performer and behind the scenes as a serial entrepreneur. I was curious to learn from Lloyd about what daily routines have worked for him.

> **As an artist, you will have to find the mood**

"There is no real strategy. I'm a very fluid guy: there's no similar day and every day is different, except my duties to my family. For my work I just have to find my rhythm, what works well. I don't fabricate things, I don't box myself, I just try to get a feel for what I can do and then do it. If I get tired, I'll just move on and do other things. So there's no such thing as, "I started this thing and I will finish it at this time." I just have to find my rhythm. If I don't feel like working, I will not work, but that seldom happens because there are just so many things to do. If you are a start-up entrepreneur, you have to find your way, you have to find the mood to do it: you have to find your rhythm.

If I'm not 100 percent in the zone, then I am going to have problems. I still have some books that are not finished yet and I jump to another project and finish it. As an entrepreneur, as my own boss, I can do that. That's the thing about art. As an artist, you will have to find the mood. You cannot paint if you're not in the mood, you cannot sing a song if you're not in the mood for music. In the same way, you cannot force yourself to write. The challenge is how to find your mood.

Daily inspiration is so important. If you don't get enough inspiration for a day, you probably won't finish a chapter. After a certain amount of words, call it a day and go back to your family, play with your kids and have some dinner with your wife and family and sleep well. Kiss them good night and wake up to another day and say good morning. Find other things to inspire you to write the next chapter. I think it's about finding daily inspiration

> **It's about finding daily inspiration in little things: looking at the things that give you a positive perspective**

in little things, looking at the things that give you a positive perspective. If you are stuck in traffic, you have to ask, 'What can I do in a traffic situation, other than blaming the traffic for this misfortune?' Just find some inspiration. It could be music, there are so many ways to be inspired, you just have to find them."

Mark Ruiz — Founder, Hapinoy

Mark Ruiz is the president and co-founder of Hapinoy: a social enterprise that empowers 'nanays' to create thriving and sustainable sari-sari stores. Mark's passion is harnessing innovation for a better world. This is evident in all the ventures he pursues. Mark shared with me the power of journaling.

"I keep a daily journal. Every single morning, with a cup of coffee in my hand, I open my laptop and get on my journal. The journal I use is an app called Day 1, It's very powerful because it works across all my devices. What I basically do is that I look at my calendar for the previous day and just go over the events of the day. It's like: this is what happened in the morning and these are the thoughts that came up.

It's just easy to say 'okay, I went to a meeting' or 'I had dinner with my wife' or 'I had lunch with a business partner.' What I try to show in my journal are the thoughts and reflections I had during specific activities and events. And I try to be conscious of why I did certain things or how I reacted to certain events, and really learn from that.

> I think that putting thoughts and experiences to paper, in this case, digital paper, helps you commit to more.

After doing this for a couple of years, it comes a little bit more naturally. If I come across journal entries that say, 'Oh why did I do that? Why did I say that? What would I do *differently?', I reflect upon how I might approach something in a new way. I think that putting thoughts and experiences to paper, in this case, digital paper, helps you commit to more. I go over the days' events – my thoughts, motivations, what worked and what I would do differently.*

One of my favorite quotes is: "No amount of walking on the wrong road will take you where you want to go". That's just so striking and it captures everything about my life. You really have to know yourself and that's not as easy as it sounds. The habit of journaling has really helped me know myself. It helps you to dig deep because sometimes things are easy to miss. Spend that time really, really digging into yourself. Be very honest about who you are and, more importantly, be very honest about what your weaknesses are. Know yourself: it's a cliché but it is the most critical basic step to your success."

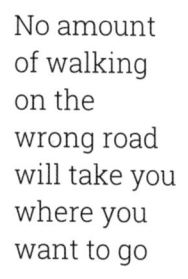

> No amount of walking on the wrong road will take you where you want to go

Powerful Lesson # 6

The secret to your success is found in your daily routine

The secret to your success is found in your daily routine. I believe in this so much that I am going to make a big statement here. You will never change your life unless you change what you do daily. I can't be more direct with you. You must commit to creating intentional daily victories in your day that make you better. The philosophy is very simple: 1% better every day. This is one of the most important messages I give to almost every single audience that I speak to, be it professional athletes, college students or seasoned executives. The same principle applies to you. No exceptions. The small daily victories *do* matter.

For a long time, I thought that the topic of my first book would be about your daily victories. I am so passionate on this topic, I could have written a series of books about it. I have benefited so much – physically, mentally, emotionally and spiritually - from the success habits that I practice today. For sure, I would not have been able to write this book without committing to these daily disciplines. But, regardless of where you are in your life, there is always the opportunity and need for you to get to the next level. That starts with the daily victory. So let me give you the 5 Minute Challenge for this chapter.

You don't learn from experience. You learn from reflecting on experience. Journaling your thoughts is the most powerful tool you can use to self reflect. Of all the daily habits I practice, perhaps the most powerful one is my morning and evening journaling exercise, "The 5-2-Win Exercise". So, depending on what time of day it is that you are reading this, I want you to complete this very short and simple writing exercise. I am just going to ask you to answer two questions. The questions are extraordinarily powerful. Leveraging the science of positive psychology and proactive thinking, I would go as far as to say that I can't think of four better questions to ask yourself on a daily basis. I want you to experience this power directly yourself.

The 5 Minute Challenge

If you are reading this in the morning or early afternoon, please answer the below two questions:

AM — beginning of day
What 3 things am I grateful for right now?
What 3 things can I do to make today great?

If you are reading this in the late afternoon or in the evening, please answer the below two questions:

PM — end of day
What 3 things were amazing about today?
What 3 things could I have done differently?

How do you feel after doing the exercise?

Let's see what **Lucy** and Diego have written first

The 5 Minute Challenge – *Lucy* & *Diego*

Lucy (reading at night)	Diego (reading at morning)
What 3 things were amazing about today?	What 3 things am I grateful for right now?
- Seeing my daughter after work and listening to her as she told me about her day. - The compliment I got from my work colleague about how I helped him complete the project - The delicious merienda I ate today	- that my friend Mary cared so much about me to buy me this book - that I played basketball with my friends last night - that I live in a comfortable home, not many people in this city can say that

What 3 things could I have done differently?	What 3 things can I do to make today great?
- Woken up earlier so that I could have prepared for my day better - I could have washed the dishes myself instead of letting mom do it again. - Not eat so much "kwek kwek" ☺ haha	- complete the client report today - eat a healthy lunch - send an email of thanks to my high school music teacher – I guess I never told him how much he influenced my life

How do you feel after doing this exercise?	
- I've never done something like this before, I have always considered myself grateful when I pray but writing it down is completely different. This is cool	- I like this one. Very simple. The power of the little things I guess, feeling very intentional

The 5 Minute Challenge - Your Turn!

PM questions — *if reading at night or late afternoon*	AM Questions — *if reading in the morning or early afternoon*
What 3 things were amazing about today?	What 3 things am I grateful for right now?
What 3 things could I have done differently?	What 3 things can I do to make today great?

How do you feel after doing this exercise?

A Note from Mike...

Congratulations! You have completed your daily victory. You have improved by 1% today. I am so excited for you. Now, imagine doing something like this every day. Think of what type of power this can create within you. At the end of this book I will talk more about how you can do this.

CHAPTER 7

You were Born for Greatness

You have been lied to. You have been abused. You have been exploited. You have been told that you are not good enough, that you are not smart enough. You have been told that, because of your past, you don't deserve a good future. You have been told that you are too small, too fat or too weak to make it on this team. You have been told that you're not beautiful enough, that you are too brown, that you will never be a beauty queen. You are told that you're too stupid to get a job, too dumb to be promoted.

You have been told that, because of your family's background, you will never make it big, and you will never amount to anything. You have been told that, because of the mistakes of your past, you will never have the abundant future you dream of. You have been told, because of your sexual preferences, that you are not normal and are a freak. You have been told, because of your choice of religion, that you are not welcome here, that you are an outcast. You have been told that if you were born poor you will die poor.

> You have been lied to

You have been told that, because you don't go to the so-called 'best school', you will never reach the top of your profession. You have been told you don't deserve the same level of service and respect that a foreigner commands. You have been told that, because you don't have a bank account or a debit card, you are not a respected member of society. You have been told that success is only for the few and that happiness is only for the lucky. You have been told that you are not worthy of great things. Worst of all you have been told that you are powerless to change anything.

> Never, *ever* let someone else's opinion of you define who you are.

I am here to tell you that these things you have been told are lies. They are not true. Never, *ever* let someone else's opinion of you define who you are. Never, *ever* let someone else's limited beliefs define how you think. Never, *ever* let someone else's flawed assumptions define your reality. Whether that person is a celebrity, a boss, a best friend, a parent, a teacher, or a sibling. Those negative words were not meant for you. That is not who you are. That is not part of your reality.

Powerful Lesson #7
Don't believe the lies. You were born for greatness

You were born to become world-class. You were born to unleash your potential. You were born to realize your greatness. An extraordinary amount of power lies within you. It can't even be measured. It is limitless. Remember, you are part of the human race. We are the greatest species that was ever created. You, like every other member of humanity, have the ability to be aware of who you are, the ability to visualize a better future, the ability to make the decision to take control of your life and the ability to have an inner voice to guide you on your journey. These are gifts that no animal has. This is what makes you and I uniquely human.

As we come to the end of this book, I ask you to reflect deeply over the next few pages. You will read the final words of wisdom written by the 21 amazing world-class Filipinos who made this book possible. You have read their stories, now I ask you to reflect deeply over their final words. I am convinced that there will be at least one quote that was written specifically for you. A message that you need to hear. A message that you need to hear right now, to help you overcome a challenge, to help you to keep moving forward, to help you to still believe. Remember this book was written for you. These words are for you.

"Make yourself so valuable that people can't afford to lose you"

— Josh Mahinay

"You must be intentional, seek knowledge, seek truth"

— Francis Kong

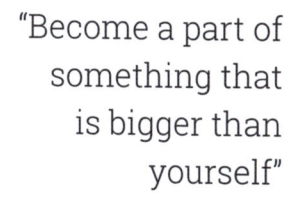

"Become a part of something that is bigger than yourself"

— Krie Reyes-Lopez

"Never forget: you have worth, you have dignity, you have purpose"

— Anna Meloto-Wilk

"Happiness is a choice: choose to be happy. Life is hard and difficult but you have a choice: choose to be happy"

— Rey Bufi

"You are part of the generation that is tasked to bring the Philippines to a first world country and I believe that we will see it in our lifetime"

— Anton Diaz

"Be genuine,
be remarkable,
be someone people
want to connect with"

— Ginger Arboleda

"Continue building on what you're strong at, strengthen whatever your strength is, rather than spreading yourself out too thinly"

— Steve Benitez

"As long as you keep on doing what is good, what is right, what is loving, you will win, you will win, you will win"

— Marianne Mencias

"You don't have to do great things to help people. You don't have to be rich to help the poor. You just need to have the heart"

— Benjie Abad

"There is a purpose to your life, and by discovering that purpose, you will find happiness and that's a gift that no one can steal from you"

— Tony Meloto

"The definition of success is making the difference. It's not about money, it's not about material things, but how you inspire people, how you help them, how you can touch them, what you can do for them"

— Rebecca Bustamante

"Join God where He is already at work"

— Boris Joaquin

"Success doesn't mean you are rich and famous, success is all about making other people better and happy"

— Pocholo Gonzales

"Stay true to what you believe in, stay true to yourself, but don't be satisfied. Keep going, continue to grow"

— Noey Lopez

"Whatever you want to do, if you tell the universe what you want, the universe will give it to you"

— Vince Golangco

"If you search deep in your hearts, you are created with so much good, you have such a capacity to do good. Let's not believe it when the world says otherwise"

— Issa Cuevas-Santos

"If you want to be loved in a certain way, first make sure that you're loving the people around you in a certain way"

— David Bonifacio

"It is not what happens to you that is important, but it is your response to what happens to you that is everything"

— Mark Ruiz

"Focus on progress, not perfection"

— Marv De Leon

"The best time to believe in yourself is when nobody else believes in you"

— Lloyd Luna

Listen to the full interviews today!

INSPIRING FILIPINO EXCELLENCE

Subscribe now for FREE!

www.mikegrogan.ph/podcast

Best of You

THE PHILIPPINES' NO. 1 SUCCESS PODCAST

Subscribe on iTunes   Subscribe on Stitcher

The 5 Minute Challenge

Pick an area in your life that you want to improve the most. An area of your life that you need to take to the next level. An area of your life that you know needs your attention right now (for example, your personal health, a family relationship, your career, your spiritual journey, your business, your passion.)

Now, create as many positive self beliefs (affirmations) as you can for that area of your life. Remember: self belief is the first step of greatness; it is the first step towards unleashing your potential. It is the first step towards realizing your greatness. You are doing this for a reason. There is a voice inside you telling you how powerful you are. Listen to it.

Lastly, I want you to make a promise to yourself. Not to me or anyone else but to yourself. I want you to think of three concrete positive behaviors, either an existing positive behavior or a new positive behavior that you can do to improve this area of your life. I then want you to make a commitment to doing that behavior. Remember: words without action are meaningless. Thoughts without follow through are worthless. Saying is not enough, you must do.

Let's see what Lucy and Diego have written first.

The 5 Minute Challenge – *Lucy* and *Diego*

Lucy

Area of Focus (role): *Career*
Your Positive Beliefs:
I am smart
I am dedicated.
I am a positive influence
I am disciplined
I am energetic
I am capable of running my own business one day

> **Your Promise to yourself:**
>
> I am committed to always dedicating time every day to learning something that will make me a better person.
>
> I am committed to helping a team member every day at work solve a problem
>
> I am committed to bringing a healthy snack to work every day to help me have more energy and be more creative

How do you feel after completing the exercise?

Wow this is so inspiring!!

I feel so confident after doing this.

I am excited to share this with my friends.

Diego

Area of Focus (role): *Musician*

Your Positive Beliefs:

> I am a rock star
>
> I am an artist
>
> I am a performer
>
> I am child of music
>
> I am greatly loved
>
> I am a music teacher

Your Promise to yourself:

> I am committed to continue practicing my guitar every day this week until I am able to play "Stairway to Heaven" from memory.
>
> I am committed to listening to my teacher's audio tapes every morning on the way to work to improve my music ear.
>
> I am committed to dedicating 1 hour every Sunday to help my younger cousin learn the guitar.

> **How do you feel after completing the exercise?**
>
> *I love this exercise. This was the most inspiring one for me. Feeling very powerful right now. Can't believe I'm almost at the end of this book.*

The 5 Minute Challenge - Your Turn!

Area of Focus (role):
Your Positive Beliefs: I am
Your Promise to yourself: I am committed to

> **How do you feel after doing this exercise?**

A Note from Mike...

> The biggest problem in the world is not the gap between knowing and not knowing. The biggest problem in the world is between knowing and doing. Thank you for appreciating the importance of completing the 5 Minute Challenge for this chapter. Greatness awaits you.

Your Final Challenge

I am convinced that it is now clear to you that success is a choice. Becoming world-class is a choice. Unleashing your potential is a choice. Realizing your greatness is a choice. The good news is that you are the one who makes that choice, no one else.

The other good news is that success is a journey. Becoming world-class is a journey. Unleashing your potential is a journey. Realizing your greatness is a journey. I believe that, after finishing this book, you will have proven that you are one of the people already on your way to success. I take it as my responsibility to help you as best I can.

But you finishing this book is just one tiny piece of your story. The story of how you realized your greatness. The story of how you unleashed your potential. The story of how you became a world-class Filipino. I am now inviting you to come with me to the next level.

I am going to give you one final challenge: the 40 day challenge. I believe with all my heart that, if you fully embrace this challenge, it will change your life forever. Remember: knowing without doing is not knowing. Understanding without doing is not understanding. Learning without doing is not learning. Dare to be better than yesterday. I know you can do it. I believe in you.

The 40 Day Challenge

The 40 Day Challenge is designed to help you create a proven success habit in your life that I guarantee will make you become more productive, more happy and more effective. This is the most powerful success habit that I practice: The 5-2-Win Exercise {5 minutes to answer 2 questions for your daily win}. I have seen it change my life and the lives of countless others around the world. It is a world-class habit. I know, if you fully embrace it, it will also change your life.

The practice is very simple. It is a journaling practice that you complete at the beginning and at the end of the day. It should take you no more than five minutes to complete.

Successful people are simply those with successful habits

At the beginning of the day (AM) you answer the below two questions.

- ❋ What 3 things am I grateful for right now?
- ❋ What 3 things can I do to make today great?

At the end of the day (PM) you answer the below two questions.

- ❋ What 3 things were amazing about today?
- ❋ What 3 things could I have done differently?

You can write the answers in your notebook, on your phone or your computer. It doesn't matter. As long as you write it down. Within a few days of doing it, you will directly experience and feel the benefit of the practice. I want you to repeat this exercise for 40 days. This will be enough time for this exercise to become a habit. To help you be successful in this final challenge, I have attached a simple checklist. I have used this in the past to help me create success habits in my life. This is a tool to help you. Once the exercise becomes a habit, you won't need a checklist – the practice will become automatic.

For this challenge, I want to ask you to find someone who you can share this journey with. I can't stress enough the importance of sharing and learning from others. That was the purpose of Lucy and Diego contributing to this book. Because they shared, it helped you answer each of the challenge questions. I want you to find someone to share this journey with. It may be a friend, a work colleague or a family member.

To significantly increase the likelihood of you being successful with this challenge, I have prepared six powerful questions that I want you to answer before you start. As always, and for the final time, Lucy and Diego will share their answers.

The 40 Day Challenge – Lucy and Diego

Lucy	Diego
Are you committed to completing the 40 day challenge ?	
Yes. I am committed to completing this challenge.	Definitely. I am going to do this.
How will you do it ?	
I will use my notebook and favorite pen	I will use my computer.
Where are you going to do it ?	
Morning: In my bedroom Night: On the sofa in the family room	Morning: At my desk in my office. Night: In my bedroom
When exactly (after X, before Y, during Z) ?	
Morning: After I brush my hair in the mirror and before I go downstairs to cook breakfast. Night: When my family are watching the 9pm evening news on TV and before I go upstairs for bed	Morning: After I get my morning coffee and before I open up my email. Night: After I brush my teeth and before I go to sleep
Who is going to help you ?	
I am going to tell my best friend Jane about this. I want her to do it too. I can't wait to share with her.	To be honest, I want to complete this first myself before sharing it with anyone. I will join "**The Rise of the Pinoy**" Facebook Group though. I think I will learn a lot from seeing how others are progressing.
Why do you want to do this ?	
To be a better person. I am really inspired by the World-Class Filipinos in the book. I want to become a world-class Filipino ☺	I want to prove to myself that I can develop this success habit. I am fed up of the feeling that I am not living my life to my potential. This book really changed me. 1% better everyday. Yeah I want this.

To learn how other readers are completing "The 40 day Challenge" join "The Rise of the Pinoy Community" on Facebook.

| f | The Rise of the Pinoy Community 🔍 |

Now it's your turn. I know you can be successful. There is power in your answers.

The 40 Day Challenge – Your Turn!

Are you committed to completing the 40 day challenge ?

How will you do it ?

Where are you going to do it ?

When exactly (after X, before Y, during Z) ?

Who is going to help you ?

Why do you want to do this ?

My 40 Day Challenge Checklist ✓

	Day 1	Day 2	Day 3	Day 4	Day 5	Day 6	Day 7	Day 8	Day 9	Day 10
AM										
PM										

	Day 11	Day 12	Day 13	Day 14	Day 15	Day 16	Day 17	Day 18	Day 19	Day 20
AM										
PM										

	Day 21	Day 22	Day 23	Day 24	Day 25	Day 26	Day 27	Day 28	Day 29	Day 30
AM										
PM										

	Day 31	Day 32	Day 33	Day 34	Day 35	Day 36	Day 37	Day 38	Day 39	Day 40
AM										
PM										

✓ AM — Beginning of Day
3 Things I am grateful for
3 Things I can do to make today great

✓ PM — End of Day
3 Amazing Things that happened today
3 Things I could have done differently

A Final Note from Mike...

We have now come to the end of this book. I can't thank you enough for taking the time to read it. This book really was written for *you*. I wish you success in everything you do. I know you will be successful in completing the 40 day challenge. I believe in you. I have faith in you. This is the beginning of your personal transformation. You will never be the same again. This is the beginning of a new you.

Book Summary

The 7 Powerful Lessons of Success from 21 WORLD-CLASS FILIPINOS

1   Be reminded of your inspiration daily

2   You have a unique assignment that only you can complete

3   If your motive is wrong, nothing can be right

4   The quality of the questions you ask yourself will determine your destiny

5   Embracing your pain qualifies you to be of greater service to a greater number of people

6   The secret to your success is found in your daily routine

#7   Don't believe the lies. You were born for greatness

Epilogue

Every day, people ask me why I choose to live in the Philippines. I tell them: ask me an even better question. Why am I choosing to *stay* in the Philippines? The answer is because I believe in the Filipino. I believe in the Philippines. I believe in you. Your people have given so much value to other nations of the world by the care and commitment of millions of OFWs. Your heroes have sacrificed so much to one day see a nation not only free from the oppression of a foreign nation, but also free from the false beliefs that are holding you back from greatness.

"I die without seeing the dawn brighten over my native land. You who have it to see, welcome it – and forget not those who have fallen during the night."

— Jose Rizal

The time has now come for the vision of Rizal to be realized. For you are the generation called to create a First World Philippines in our lifetime. To create a nation where no one will be left behind. To work together to build a "walang iwanan" economy that will create abundance for all, motivated by love of family, country and the rest of humanity. The unique assignment you have been given is a part of this greater future. The nation, and the world, is less without your light. We need your light to shine.

With all my heart, I tell you the truth. This book was written for you. I know that it is not a coincidence that I wrote this book. This book is a part of your story. It really was written for you; to inspire and empower you; to renew your mind; to restore your sight; to give you strength; to give you courage; to set you free from those who try to oppress you. The time for your personal transformation is now. The rise of the Pinoy has already begun. Now what are you going to do?

Acknowledgements

So many people to say thanks to. This book was not the work of one person. It takes a team of people to create it.

I want to thank the 21 World-Class Filipinos that were interviewed for this book. Thank you for your time, vulnerability and wisdom.

Mary Grace Gabaya, my lead thinking partner for this book and my number one fan. I could not have done it without you.

To Malcolm and Jocelyn Pick, your faith in me, made all of this possible.

Nica Mandigma, Jesie Jamoles Jaleco, Joselle Pablo and Dustin Silverio. You were with me from the very beginning. Your dedication and talent is something I greatly value.

Dok Pavia, Penelope Cabot and Ian Perez. Your creative genius made these pages look so much better.

The staff, past and present of CCBRT, Tanzania. My time with you has forever inspired me to work for the greater good.

My amazing life long friends: John Paul Mantey, Seth Parsons, Mike Bull, Declan Murray, Michael Lucey, Louise Jones, Marek Dudziak, Joel Gross, Ross McMahon, Tom Vanneste, Kevin McCourt, Fulgence Lwiza, Matt Wahl, Ricky Teehan, Marc Daubenbuechel, Joe Hennelly, Emili Whittaker, Dermot Cawley, Ruben Chaumont, Tom Graham, Goodluck Malleko. You empower me to remember the great joy that is found in life.

My inspiring mentors: Kunbi Rudnick, Gordon Jonas, Richard Binns, Erik Hager, Jake Rainwater, Bob McCulley, Jim Donald, Erwin Telemans, Jim Nicolas, Brian Lane, Shirley Maya Tan, Dr. Brenda D'Mello, Charles Duffert. You constantly inspire me to greatness.

My parents, Padraic and Marie, my siblings, Lorraine, Olivia and Gregory, you are the greatest gift I ever got in life. I hope I will always make you proud.

Lucy and Diego, we changed your names to protect your identity, but I can't thank you enough for sharing your journey with us.

Surprise! There is a hidden chapter!
Download it today at www.mikegrogan.ph/hiddenchapter

Finally, you the reader. You did it, you finished the book, I'm so proud of you. Your greatest days are ahead. Thank You.

About the Author

Mike Grogan is an Irish Motivational Speaker committed to inspiring Filipino Excellence. After traveling in over 30 countries, Mike decided to make the Philippines his home. He believes in the extraordinary potential of the Filipino, and he is convinced that this is the generation that will see a First World Philippines in our Lifetime. Mike has a degree in Chemical Engineering from the University College Dublin, is a certified Lean Six Sigma Black Belt and an internationally recognized expert in Lean Management Implementation. He lives in Metro Manila and works as a speaker, coach and trainer for audiences and organizations across the Philippines.

mike | grogan

INSPIRING FILIPINO EXCELLENCE

To get in contact with Mike please visit **www.mikegrogan.ph**

or email him directly at
mike@bestofyou.ph

One Last Thing

Thank you for reading **The Rise of the Pinoy**. Getting this book into the hands of Filipinos around the world, will rely mostly on word-of-mouth. So if you have the time and inclination, please consider leaving a short review at **www.amazon.com**, **www.goodreads.com** or any other appropriate online platform.

Thank you so much for your support! ☺

Growing up
in Ireland

My Amazing Friends

Working in the Philippines

My Filipino Dream

mike | grogan
INSPIRING FILIPINO EXCELLENCE